Quilts from the Heart

• Quick Projects for Generous Giving •

KARIN RENAUD

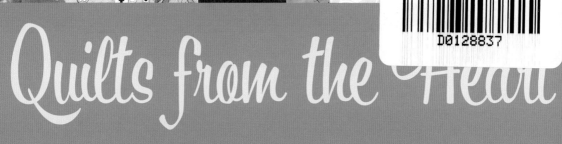

Martingale®
& COMPANY

Quilts from the Heart:
Quick Projects for Generous Giving
© 2006 by Karin Renaud

That Patchwork Place® is an imprint
of Martingale & Company®.

Martingale & Company
20205 144th Avenue NE
Woodinville, WA 98072-8478 USA
www.martingale-pub.com

Printed in China
11 10 09 08 07 06   8 7 6 5 4 3 2 1

Library of Congress Cataloging-in-Publication Data
Renaud, Karin.
    Quilts from the heart : quick projects for generous
giving / Karin Renaud.
        p. cm.
    ISBN 1-56477-649-2
    1. Quilting—Patterns. 2. Patchwork—Patterns. 3.
Children's quilts. 4. Gifts. I. Title.
    TT835.R456 2006
    746.46'041—dc22
                                            2005022832

Dedication

To Kelly Kampmann and my mother-in-law,
Margaret Renaud, who took a casual wish and
turned it into a lifelong passion. Thanks for helping me make my first quilt!

To my family for always saying they liked it.

Credits

President • Nancy J. Martin
CEO • Daniel J. Martin
VP and General Manager • Tom Wierzbicki
Publisher • Jane Hamada
Editorial Director • Mary V. Green
Managing Editor • Tina Cook
Technical Editor • Dawn Anderson
Copy Editor • Durby Peterson
Design Director • Stan Green
Illustrator • Laurel Strand
Cover and Text Designer • Regina Girard
Photographer • Brent Kane

Mission Statement

*Dedicated to providing quality products
and service to inspire creativity.*

Contents

Projects

"... for we put the thought of all that we love into all that we make."
—J.R.R. Tolkien

In August 2001 I found a copy of the South Puget Sound Project Linus newsletter at a local quilt store. Reading it, I learned that Project Linus is an organization that delivers security blankets to ill or traumatized children. The idea of making quilts for kids appealed to me, and I was moved by the letters from parents, social workers, and nurses who told how much the blankets helped.

In the past three years, I've made and donated 30 quilts to Project Linus. Each quilt has been a gift to someone I don't know and will never meet. I can only hope each person will feel better for having received it.

I've also received something with each quilt I donated. When I make quilts to give away, I can experiment and have fun! With these quilts I have permission to use colors that would never go in my house. I can try a new skill without having to make a huge quilt, or I can try out a pattern to see if it looks as good completed as it did in my head.

Making a quilt for donation provides me the opportunity to buy a wonderful novelty fabric, even though my kids are now too old for it and my friends don't need it because they're done having babies. It gives me joy to drop off a quilt for pickup and imagine the look on a child's face as he or she sees it for the first time and realizes it's for keeping.

Because I've found making quilts for Project Linus so rewarding, I put together this book of fun, kid-friendly quilt patterns. The quilts all fall within the general guidelines of many charity organizations, including Project Linus (see page 6). They can be done in any fabric combination that you choose and, if you're willing to do a little math, in any size you want. I hope you'll consider making one or more to donate to Project Linus or a charity of your choice.

My hope for all my quilts isn't that they become heirlooms, but that they die of old age from many washings and much love. I hope each one is used as a picnic table, fort, Superman's cape, or magic carpet, and yes, maybe even as a blanket.

Making a Quilt to Donate

In western Washington State, where I live, there are many nonprofit groups that accept quilts. Domestic violence organizations, homeless shelters, transitional housing programs, nursing homes, pediatric care centers for drug-affected infants, and hospitals are all institutions to which you could donate a quilt.

The best way to find an organization in your area is to contact your local quilt shop or guild. They are often involved in community service projects and would be able to direct you to an appropriate person. You could also make phone calls to local hospitals or community service agencies in your area. See page 95 for a list of some of the many organizations that accept donated quilts.

Before making a quilt for a specific charitable organization, contact that organization for guidelines. Most charitable groups have rules regarding acceptable colors, sizes, and fiber content, among other things.

Many community-service organizations are 501(c)(3) nonprofit corporations, and are eligible to receive tax-deductible contributions. Consult your tax advisor to determine the deductibility of any gift.

Organizing a Quilting Bee

In addition to donating quilts as an individual, it can be a great deal of fun to do so as part of a group. The group can be an informal gathering of friends who make quilts to donate, or it can be a larger, more formal group. Churches, youth groups, clubs, and schools can all be great places to find quiltmakers. Quilt shops are often willing to let people use their classrooms to sew when they aren't in use.

Organizing a group to make quilts doesn't have to be difficult, and can in fact be a great deal of fun. You'll have to consider a few things before you begin.

- What is the skill level of the quilters who are participating?
- How many people can you fit into the space you have available?
- Are you going to pool your materials and work together, or will each quilter work independently at the same time?
- Who is going to be responsible for unfinished projects?
- Who is going to be responsible for setup and cleanup?
- And, most importantly, who is bringing snacks?

The answers to these questions will help define what you need to do. If you have novice sewers, or people who don't sew but want to help, pooling materials and using precut kits with step-by-step directions is probably the best way to go. This will allow everyone to be involved, and you'll end up with fewer partially done projects. The coordinator, or those who are more experienced, will probably be required to do any finishing work.

If you have a group of experienced quilters, then each person might wish to work independently but together as a group. In that case, each individual will probably be responsible for finishing his or her own work.

Both these types of gatherings can result in wonderful quilts and be a lot of fun. It's exciting to watch someone who's never made a quilt before see things come together. The key thing to remember, in either case, is to have something for everyone to do and to make sure that you keep expectations realistic. It's better to make two or three beautiful quilts than eight or nine unfinished projects.

Project Linus

Project Linus is a 100%-volunteer organization established in 1995. Karen Loucks read about a little girl whose "blankie" helped her through painful cancer treatments. Karen decided to begin gathering security blankets for other children, and Project Linus was begun.

Over the past 10 years, Project Linus has expanded from one woman collecting blankets for children with cancer to 371 chapters in the United States. As of July 2004 Project Linus had given over one million handmade quilts, afghans, and blankets to children in need.

In its 10-year existence, Project Linus has grown from a group serving cancer patients in the Denver area to an organization helping children throughout the country. The children it serves are ill, have experienced abuse, or have suffered some type of trauma. The organizations that Project Linus serves are as varied as each of its different chapters.

For more information about Project Linus or to find a chapter near you, visit their Web site at www.projectlinus.org.

Following are the national Project Linus guidelines. Although individual Project Linus chapters and other organization guidelines may vary, this list provides a general idea of what is accepted.

- Project Linus welcomes any handmade quilt, as well as knitted and crocheted blankets.
- Blankets must be machine washable and dryable.
- Blankets need to be in kid-friendly colors. Darker colors are okay for the youth blankets.
- Any size handmade blanket is welcome, with a suggested range of 36" x 36" to twin-sized.
- It is important that there are no pins, strings, or tails accidentally left attached to the blanket.
- Please make sure there is no odor, especially cigarette smoke or fabric softener, lingering in the blanket.
- Blankets with mold or mildew can't be accepted.

Project Linus quilts have had a profound impact on the lives of children and their families. Whenever I turn in a quilt for donation, I think of some of the letters I've read in the South Puget Sound Project Linus newsletter. Two examples are below.

Lynn at Project Linus:

I took the donated blankets from Project Linus to children in our intensive care unit a few minutes ago. One toddler's mom got teary when I told her it was Matthew's to keep. This family is from southwest Washington. They see Tacoma as a "big city" and expected people at the hospital to be all businesslike. I wish I could remember their exact words of kindness about how supported and good they feel about their experience here. The mom's name is Shelly and she asked me to personally thank you for the blanket!!!

So there it is. As usual, I just wish all the sewers, knitters, and crocheters could be here to see the pleasure and appreciation in people's eyes when they receive the blankets.

Again, thanks.

Joan

To Project Linus:

I just wanted to say thank you to the Project Linus group. On June 5th, my daughter had a four-hour surgery at Mary Bridge [Children's Hospital and Health Center]. When we got back to the room, she told the nurse she was cold. The nurse came back with a beautiful quilt from Project Linus. Since we have gotten home, my daughter has not gone to bed without it one time. She may be 17 years old, but she still is a little one who knows what a treasure this was to receive while in the hospital.

Again, thank you, Project Linus.

Sabrina M.

The blocks that are the basis for the quilts in this book are all traditional patterns. They are known by many names and have been around for decades. I love the history that is a part of quilting. I'm continually looking through Barbara Brackman's *Encyclopedia of Pieced Quilt Patterns* (which my husband refers to as my "quilt-nerd book") trying new patterns and designs. I love the thought that my great-grandmother might have pieced a Shoo Fly block more than 100 years ago, and that I can teach someone else to make it today.

The simple structure and repetition of the blocks provides the foundation for the quilt. The simplicity allows for an incredible amount of flexibility in the fabric choices. The blocks can stand alone and don't require continuity of color to hold the quilt together. As a result, these traditional patterns lend themselves well to my favorite type of quilts: scrap quilts.

Scrap Quilts

There are a variety of ways to make scrap quilts. Random scrap quilts often use fabrics more than once. "Snowball" (page 74) and "Arkansas Cross-roads" (page 26) are examples of random scrap quilts. In these quilts, the blocks were constructed of randomly placed bright fabrics and a background fabric.

Another type of scrap quilt uses a wide variety of fabrics, but they are placed specifically. In "Churn Dash" (page 42) and "Unequal Irish Chain" (page 88) each block is made up of just two fabrics: the background and a bright print. This type of quilt has a much more structured feel than a random scrap quilt. The idea is taken a step further in "Block in a Box," (page 29), where the fabrics used in each block are all in the same color family.

The last type of scrap quilt is actually a blending of a structured fabric design and a random scrap quilt. Quilts like "Farmer's Flowers" (page 46) and "Lincoln's Platform" (page 56) have specific fabrics in some areas and random fabrics in others. The blending of the different types of fabric placement allows you to emphasize different areas of the quilt. The simple elegance of these traditional patterns truly allows you to do anything you might want to try.

Tip

If you're making a quilt from a limited number of fabrics and you want to make sure the fabrics will visually blend in the finished quilt, put scraps of each fabric into a glass jar. Look at them all mixed up. If one fabric stands out, you can decide if you want to include it or not. The same can be true for looking at a fabric that you do want to stand out. If it doesn't stand out from the other fabrics in the jar, you might want to choose a different fabric.

Pattern Options

The structure that allows for a variety of different fabric choices also makes it easy to adapt the blocks and patterns in this book to create an amazing variety of quilts. Many of the blocks used are the same size, with the most common size being 6". In addition to making the single-block quilts shown in the book, you can combine any similarly sized blocks to create a new and unique quilt.

Changing the location of the white and bright-colored fabrics within a quilt can also change the feel of the design. The X blocks and O blocks in "X's and O's" (page 92) are stitched together in exactly the same way. The only difference between the blocks is where the white is placed. The addition, or removal, of sashing strips can change the feel as well. Adding white sashing can make a tightly packed quilt feel airy, while adding a bright-colored sashing can add intensity.

Background fabric can also change the feel of the quilt. Although black fabric isn't suggested for quilts you plan to donate, it can be used to make bright colors stand out. It gives a quilt more of a traditional Amish feeling.

Skill Level

All the quilts in this book were designed with a beginning or novice quilter in mind. The increasing skill levels indicate an increase in the number of steps required to complete the quilt and/or that the quilt may contain a significant number of small pieces.

The Project Instructions

Each project is written in a similar format. The first section lists the finished sizes of the blocks, sashing, and borders. Don't use these general measurements when cutting fabric. They are for your reference if you decide to change the size of the quilt.

Materials

The fabric requirement is the yardage that is needed to complete each quilt as shown. If you want to change the size of a quilt (see page 22), you can determine how much fabric you'll need by adding up the amount of fabric required for each piece of the same color and then adding 10% to allow a cushion for error. Round up to the nearest ⅛ yard.

Single Block Requirements

The single block requirements list what you'd need to make a single block of a given design. If you're going to make a quilt where each block is made of a different fabric, such as "Shoo Fly" (page 63) or "Churn Dash" (page 42), having the piece requirements for each block is more helpful than knowing the piece requirements for the entire quilt. It's also information you'll need if you're going to change the size of your quilt.

Cutting

For each project, the cutting instructions list how many pieces of each fabric you'll need to complete the quilt as shown. It includes the number of sashing, border, and binding strips required.

This section provides you with information you'll need to get started and techniques you'll use to make and finish your quilt. It covers selecting fabric, gathering tools, cutting pieces, binding edges, and quilting.

Fabric

I use good quality 100%-cotton fabric purchased at a quilt store. With fabric, you truly do get what you pay for. If you're going to spend your time and energy making a quilt, it's better to use quality fabric that will last.

I make my donation quilts in kid-friendly hues, using primary colors in both bright and pastel tones. I avoid black and muddy colors. Novelty prints, both large and small, are fun to incorporate into your quilts. Whether it's a large fussy-cut square or a small allover print, a novelty print adds pizzazz to a project.

Gathering Fabric

Choosing fabric can be intimidating, but it can also be the most fun. I'm a *fabricaholic.* I love buying fabric just for the sake of buying fabric, which is why I love scrap quilting.

If you're a beginning quilter, you may not have a stockpile of fabrics and scraps to use when a pattern calls for "assorted fabrics." Don't let this prevent you from making scrap quilts.

There are many ways to expand your fabric collection. First of all, take advantage of the fabric you do have. If you've made any previous quilts, cut those miscellaneous leftover pieces into smaller squares the size that you require. For example, a five-inch scrap square will give you four 2½" squares of fabric.

Purchasing quarter-yard cuts (9" x the width of the fabric) or fat quarters (18" x 22") is another excellent way to increase your fabric stash. If you want to coordinate your fabrics, many stores offer precut fabric bundles. You can then use all the different fabrics to make a single quilt or pieces of it in several quilts.

If you're sewing in a group or with a friend, mix and match your fabrics. If you each purchase eight fat quarters and split them, you now have 16 fabrics to choose from. Lastly, many magazines and online quilting sites offer to host fabric exchanges.

I'm continually expanding my quilt stash. One way I do this is by letting my children choose fabric. I love cool colors—purples, blues, greens and fuchsias. I'm not big on the reds, yellows, and oranges. My daughter's favorite color is red, and my son loves geometrics and novelty fabrics. Letting my children choose fabric not only expands the types of fabric I have, but it also allows my children to look at different quilts and say, "That's my fabric."

When I purchase fabric for a specific project, I expand my stash by buying a little extra so that I can cut it into 2½" and 3½" squares. I also save any ends from borders and sashing and cut them into squares that I'll use later. When I find a fabric that I really like, I buy some just because I like it.

Novelty fabrics

Scrap Storage

I precut fabric in 2", 2½", and 3½" squares so that when I'm putting together fabric for a scrap quilt, I don't have to spend a great deal of time cutting. I've found that a plastic desk organizer with three drawers works well for storing precut squares. The 9" x 12" drawers are big enough to hold several hundred squares, and the container itself is small enough to fit on my worktable.

Scrap organizer

Backing

Backing fabric is what goes on the back of your quilt, and it is usually a solid piece of fabric. For quilts that are up to 36" wide, you can generally use a single piece of fabric cut about 4" longer than the length of the quilt top. For quilts wider than 36" it's necessary to piece two strips of fabric together for the backing. Another option for larger quilts is fabric specifically designed to be quilt backing. Several companies make good quality 108"-wide backing fabric. The 108" backing fabric costs more per yard, but you don't have to buy nearly as much, and it's generally more cost-effective than pieced backing.

Binding

The binding is the finished edge of the quilt. When selecting your binding, there are several alternatives. The first one is to use the same fabric for your binding that you used for the final border. The binding will then blend into the top of the quilt. You can also select one of the colors in the quilt top for your binding. This will bring out the color you selected and add a band of contrasting color around the edge of the quilt. Examples of this type of binding

are "Unequal Double Irish Chain" (page 85) and "Simple Nine Patch" (page 67).

Rather than use a fabric from the quilt top for the binding, another alternative is to select a different fabric altogether. "Arkansas Crossroads" (page 26) is an example of a quilt with this type of binding. For random scrap quilts, I'll frequently choose a solid-colored binding to add a calm finish to the quilt.

It can also be fun to make the binding out of several different fabrics. "Lincoln's Platform" (page 56) is an example of pieced binding. I've found that pieced bindings are most eye-catching when the quilt isn't too busy and the outer border is a solid fabric.

Supplies

Basic supplies

Cutting tools: A rotary cutter, acrylic rulers, and a cutting mat make quilting much easier. If you're just beginning to quilt, I recommend the purchase of a medium-sized cutting mat, a 6" x 24" ruler, and a rotary cutter. In addition to my 6" x 24" ruler, I use a 6½" x 6½" or 6" x 12" ruler for cutting smaller pieces and a 6" Bias Square® Ruler from That Patchwork Place for making half-square-triangle units. If you're planning on making a quilt with half-square-triangle units, I recommend purchasing a Bias Square ruler. You may also want a second ruler for projects requiring 6½" or larger squares. Placing rulers side by side allows you to accurately measure strips or pieces that are wider than a single-ruler width (see "Cutting" on page 11).

Either a 12" x 18" or 18" x 24" cutting mat is a good size to have. Both are small enough to be portable, but large enough for you to cut large strips of fabric.

There are two basic styles of rotary cutters. One has a stick handle, the other a grip handle. I would suggest trying them out in your hand before purchasing one. I have both types and personally prefer a grip handle. It keeps my wrist and hand parallel to the fabric and is more comfortable when I'm cutting fabric for a long time.

Sewing machine: Any sewing machine can make beautiful quilts. The stitch that I use 95% of the time on my machine is the straight stitch. Make sure your machine is in good working order and that the thread tension is consistent. Tension problems can cause more frustration than nearly anything else. If you're having problems with the tension on your machine, take it into a repair shop and ask them to take a few minutes to sew with you. They can help you get the tension set correctly for your machine.

Iron: I press everything that I sew. I prefer to use a good steam iron when pressing quilts. If you have an iron that drips water, turn off the steam and use a small spray bottle to mist your fabric.

Sewing tools: Sharp pins, a seam ripper, and marking tools are always out on my sewing table. I find that 0.5-mm mechanical pencils work well for marking fabric when I'm making half-square-triangle units or Flying Geese blocks. I also have two pairs of scissors. One is a pair of very sharp sewing scissors; the other is a pair of general-use utility scissors.

Thread: I use a neutral-colored thread—cream, white, or light gray—that will blend with most fabrics.

Batting: There is a wide variety of batting available, from cotton and wool to polyester. The choice of batting is really up to you. What you choose depends upon how you plan to quilt your project, what you want to use it for, and how much you want to spend.

There are several great books on quilting your quilt. *Machine Quilting Made Easy* by Maurine Noble (Martingale & Company, 1994) is an excellent resource, not just for quilting but also for selecting the right batting for your project.

I use 100% cotton batting. I like the way it feels and drapes. Since I machine quilt all of my quilts, I don't have the needling problems that some hand quilters have with cotton.

Cutting

I cut all the fabric for a quilt before I begin to sew. Doing so allows me to have everything I need all together. I have a small work area, and by precutting, I don't have to move everything around all the time to make room for my cutting mat.

The fabric pieces in this book are all individually cut. I cut one color of fabric at a time and begin with the largest pieces of that color. This enables me to use any leftover pieces from large strips by cutting them into smaller squares. It also makes the most efficient use of the fabric. I store cut pieces together in gallon-sized ziplock bags. This method keeps pieces organized, flat, and clean.

When cutting fabric, always cut away from you.

To cut the fabric strips:

1. Fold the yardage in half, selvage to selvage, aligning the grain lines and placing the folded edge closest to you.
2. Use your rotary cutter and a long ruler to trim the left edge off your fabric. To ensure a straight cut that is perpendicular to the fold, align a square ruler with the folded edge of the fabric and place the long ruler against the left side. Remove the square ruler and cut along the right edge of the long ruler.

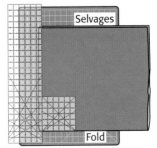

Align rulers.

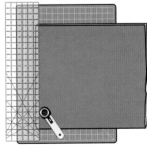

Make a clean cut.

3. Carefully measure the width of your strip with the long ruler, and cut as shown at left. If the width of your strip is wider than the width of your ruler, place two rulers side by side to ensure accurate cuts as shown at right.

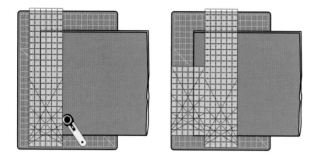

4. Cut all the strips you need before you cut the strips into individual pieces.

Cutting Pieces from a Strip

Use your rotary cutter and ruler to trim the selvage edges off the fabric strip. Measure and cut the pieces from the strip, stopping periodically to square up the left edge.

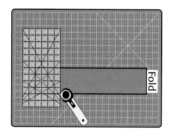

If a pattern requires rectangular pieces, I cut the strip as wide as the larger dimension of the rectangle and then cut the smaller dimension of the rectangle from the strip. For example, "Single Chain and Knot" (page 70) requires 2½" x 6½" rectangles. I cut the fabric strips 6½" wide and then cut the strips into 2½" pieces. This is generally the most efficient use of the fabric. To cut pieces wider than the width of your ruler, place two rulers side by side as shown in step 3 above.

Fussy Cutting

Fussy cutting is a technique where you select and then cut specific pieces out of the fabric, rather than just cutting straight across the fabric. Fussy cutting is generally used with novelty fabrics. It allows you to center a specific design in a prominent place in your quilt.

The process of fussy cutting is time-consuming but not difficult. Begin by deciding what design on your fabric you want to cut out. I usually choose a design at the edge of the fabric and work toward the center.

1. When fussy cutting fabric, the trick is to keep seam allowances in mind. Let's say you want to center a fabric motif in a square, and the project instructions tell you to cut the square to 3½" x 3½". That means your motif needs to fit inside a smaller 3" square, because seam allowances will eat up ¼" along each edge. To make sure the motif will fit within that 3" space, measure the motif from top to bottom and from side to side. In the fabric shown below, the animal motif measures 2" x 1¾".

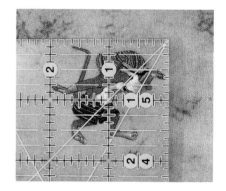

2. Center the fabric motif under a ruler. For our 3½" cut square, the center point would be 1¾", so we'd center the motif under the 1¾" intersection on the ruler.

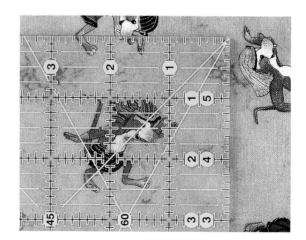

3. Cut along the edges of the ruler on the top and right sides.

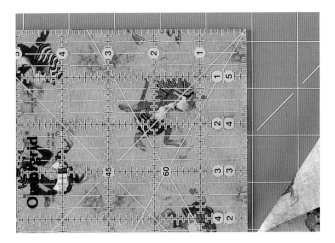

4. Rotate the fabric so that you can cut the other two sides. Align the ruler so that the two cut edges are at the 3½" line and trim the remaining sides. The design should be centered within your square.

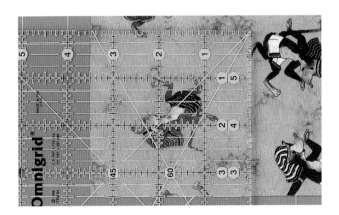

The finished fussy-cut block

Fussy cutting requires more fabric than is needed for just cutting fabric strips. If you're fussy cutting single blocks out of a variety of fabrics, this won't significantly increase the amount of fabric required to make your quilt. If, however, you're planning on cutting all your fussy-cut blocks from a single fabric, as I did in "Unequal Double Irish Chain" (page 85), you'll have to purchase a greater amount of fabric. The fabric that you select will determine how much more you'll need.

I've found it helpful to use a cardboard cutout the size of the square I need to cut; the cutout helps me determine how many pieces I can get out of my fabric. I cut a piece of cardboard the size of the required square. Old file folders or cereal boxes work well. I then cut out the center so that I have a ¼" frame.

I take the frame shopping with me and use it to audition fabric. When I find a fabric I like, I place the frame over the design (or designs). The open center allows me to see what my finished block will look like. The outer edge shows me how much of the fabric I'll lose when I cut that block.

To determine how much fabric to purchase, open the fabric out and see how many squares you can get out of a section of fabric without overlapping the blocks. Divide the number of blocks you need by the number of blocks you can get from that section of fabric. Round up the number to the nearest whole number. That is how many sections of fabric you will need. For example, suppose you can fussy cut 10 squares out of ¼ yard of the fabric you selected. The project calls for 24 squares. Divide 24 by 10 and you get 2.4. Round 2.4 up to the nearest whole number, which is 3. You will need 3 sections of fabric, ¼ yard each, or ¾ yard total, to ensure that you have enough fabric to cut your squares.

It's not unusual to have to buy double or triple the amount of fabric for fussy cutting than you'd buy if you were cutting the fabric in strips. I always round up when I'm going to fussy cut a project. The nice thing is that if I end up with extra fabric, I can always include it in another quilt.

Tip

When fussy cutting fabric, you'll be left with a lot of scraps. I keep the scraps and cut them into smaller, useable squares. Sometimes the scrap fabric contains small motifs; sometimes it's just assorted background fabric. In either case, these pieces can be fun additions to your scrap quilts.

Sewing

All the blocks in this book are sewn together using a ¼" seam allowance with the fabric pieces right sides together. Whenever I'm done sewing, I feed a small scrap of fabric under the needle and sew partway through it. The scrap fabric keeps the threads from getting tangled when I begin to sew again.

When I'm sewing a number of similar units, I chain stitch them as follows.

1. Match the fabric pieces you're going to sew, with right sides together.

2. Start stitching on a fabric scrap, stopping just before the end of the scrap. Without cutting the thread, place the first fabric pair in front of the presser foot and then sew a ¼" seam, but do not remove the pair from the machine.

3. Align the next pair in front of the presser foot. At the end of the first pair, sew immediately into the next pair, leaving a few stitches between them. Repeat until you've sewn all the pairs together.

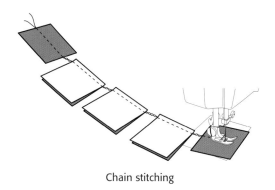

Chain stitching

4. Feed a scrap of fabric under the needle and stitch onto it. Clip the sewn blocks from behind the scrap fabric and then cut the blocks apart.

Half-Square-Triangle Units

A half-square-triangle unit is a square made up of two right triangles of different colors. Usually half-square-triangle units are constructed of a bright-colored fabric combined with a background fabric; however, they can also be constructed of two contrasting bright-colored fabrics.

There are a variety of ways to make half-square-triangle units. For scrap quilts in which I want to include the maximum variety of fabrics, I prefer the following method. Note that this technique requires a 6" Bias Square ruler.

1. Gather the fabric squares as indicated in the quilt pattern. Set aside the darker of the two fabrics.

2. Turn the lighter fabric, usually white or cream, upside down so that you're looking at the wrong side of the fabric.

3. Using a clear ruler, align the ¼" line on the ruler with the diagonal corners on the fabric square and draw a line. I use a 0.5-mm mechanical pencil. It stays sharp and leaves a nice line. Turn the

square around 180º and repeat, drawing a line ¼" from the center, parallel to the other line.

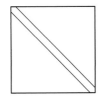

Two drawn lines,
each ¼" from the center

4. Pair the square that has the drawn lines with the darker fabric square specified in your pattern, right sides together. The lines that you drew should be on top.

5. Chain sew the squares together by sewing on the marked lines on the right side.

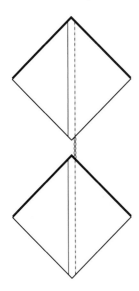

6. When you've sewn one side of all the block pairs and snipped them apart, turn the blocks around and sew on the remaining drawn line.

7. Cut the sewn squares in half, corner to corner, between the sewn lines.

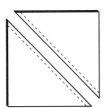

8. Press the triangles open, toward the darker fabric. There will be tabs of fabric sticking out beyond the squares.

9. The half-square-triangle units will be larger than their finished size. To trim to size, align the diagonal line on the Bias Square with the seam line on the block. The edge of the ruler should be close to the edge of the block. Trim the side and top of the block. This evens up two sides of the square.

10. Rotate the block 180º and align the diagonal line on the seam line. Align the trimmed edges of the square with the lines on the ruler that represent the finished size of the square. Trim the excess fabric off the remaining side and top edges.

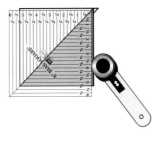

Pressing

Pressing allows pieced fabrics to lie flatter, and the overall accuracy of piecing is improved in the process. It goes hand in hand with pinning. It's much easier to pin seams when the seam allowances have been pressed.

Pressing isn't the same as ironing. Ironing is what you do to get wrinkles out of fabric; the iron moves back and forth. Pressing is what you do to make a seam allowance or pieced unit flat; the iron lifts up and down.

When I'm pressing stitched pieces, I lay multiple pieces out on my ironing pad. The "press toward" sides of the units are facing up, and the seams are on the left side of each unit.

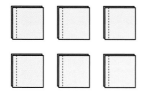

When the units are laid out, I press straight down on the seam with the iron and then pick the iron straight up and move on to the next unit. This process is called "setting the seams." When I've set the seams on all the units, I begin to press the units open, pressing toward the left side.

Here are a few general guidelines to follow when deciding which way to press your fabric.

- Press toward the darker fabric. Seam allowances can sometimes show through light fabrics.

- When pressing pieced sections, press toward the side that has the fewest seams. This will ensure that you have to sew over the fewest layers of fabric when joining blocks.

A cutting board with a towel over the top makes an excellent ironing pad. It's portable, hard, flat, and can be left set up without taking up much space.

- When beginning to sew a quilt block, notice where seams will come together and try to anticipate which direction to press pieces so seams will align. For the projects in this book, I've included "press toward" directions where it will assist in construction.

Pinning

Pinning is an important step. It increases the overall accuracy of your work and makes construction much easier. I use sharp pins and throw away any pin that is dull or bent. Dull and damaged pins are difficult to use and can damage fabric. When pinning fabrics together, I insert pins horizontally at the fabric edge, as shown below, so that I can easily pull out the pin as I sew. I leave the pin in place until just before it gets to the edge of the presser foot.

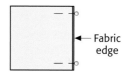

I put pins in the following places.

- Any matching seams

- The beginning and end of each section

- Every three to four inches when sewing blocks together

- Any place where the blocks don't quite meet evenly

When two pieced units are placed side by side, take care to align any seams that are supposed to meet. Matching seams is an important step because it keeps the visual line of the block unbroken. Locking seams together is the easiest way to match seams.

Locking seams takes advantage of the bulk from the seam allowances to assist in aligning seams. Doing this accurately involves a few simple steps.

1. Lay out the two sections that are going to be pinned together as they will appear on the quilt.

2. Fold the top section down over the bottom section so they are right sides together. You'll pin and sew along the top edge.

3. With the top edges aligned, begin to slide the top edges of the sections against each other horizontally until the seam allowances bump into each other. The seams are now aligned, or "locked."

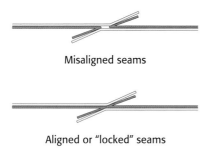

Misaligned seams

Aligned or "locked" seams

4. Pin through the center of the seam allowances to keep them aligned. If the adjoining sections have more than one matching seam, lock all the seams in the same manner.

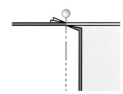

Pinning a locked seam

5. When all the seams are locked, pin the beginning and end of the sections together.

When you pin, especially on larger blocks, you might find that the sections don't match exactly. Pinning helps spread the excess fabric evenly over the length of the block to prevent large mismatched areas and big wrinkles.

If you have blocks that don't line up well, begin by pinning all the adjoining seams. This will help you determine where the blocks are mismatched. Pin the center of the excess fabric to the center of its matching piece. If the space is longer than a couple of inches, or if there is a large discrepancy between the blocks, pin again as necessary. When you sew the pieces together, leave the pins in place until they are almost under the needle. This forces the sewing machine to sew the excess fabric rather than push it toward the next pin. My personal rule of thumb is "When in doubt, pin."

Borders

For best results, measure your quilt top before cutting border strips. Because the edges of the quilt can stretch during the construction of the quilt, measure the length and width of the quilt top through the center to determine the correct length of the border strips. The borders for the quilts in this book are cut along the crosswise grain of the fabric and seamed as necessary to achieve the needed length. Because the quilts in this book are small, it is often possible to cut the top and bottom borders from one border strip, without piecing.

Straight-Cut Borders

1. Measure the width of the quilt top through the center and cut top and bottom border strips to the determined length, piecing as necessary. Mark the center of the quilt top edges and the centers of the border strips. Pin the border strips to the top and bottom edges of the quilt top, aligning ends and center marks. Using a ¼" seam allowance, stitch along the long edges and then press toward the borders. Trim any excess fabric.

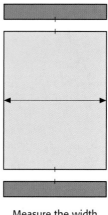

Measure the width through the center.

2. Measure the length of the quilt top through the center, including the top and bottom borders just added, and cut side border strips to the determined length, piecing as necessary. Mark the center of the quilt-top edges and the centers of the border strips. Pin the border strips to the sides of the quilt top, aligning ends and center marks. Using a ¼" seam allowance, stitch along

the long edges and then press toward the borders. Trim any excess fabric.

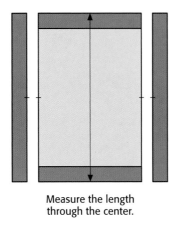

Measure the length through the center.

Borders with Corner Squares

1. Measure the width and length of the quilt top through the center and then cut border strips to the determined lengths. Piece border strips as necessary to get the needed length.

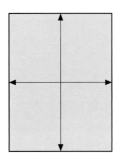

2. Mark the center of the quilt top edges on all sides and the centers of each border strip. Pin the side border strips to the sides of the quilt top, aligning ends and center marks. Using a ¼" seam allowance, stitch along the long edges and then press toward the borders.

3. Sew corner squares or pieced corner units (equal to the cut width of the border strips) to each end of the top and bottom border strips. Press seams toward the border strips. Pin the border strips to the top and bottom edges of the quilt top, matching seams. Using a ¼" seam allow-

ance, stitch along the long edges and then press toward the borders.

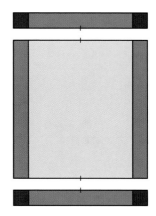

Assembling the Quilt Sandwich

When the quilt top is completed, the next step is to get it ready for quilting by assembling the quilt sandwich. Begin by ironing both the quilt top and the backing fabric. You want them to be as wrinkle-free as possible.

When both the top and backing are ironed, lay the backing fabric down on your pinning surface so that the wrong side of the backing is facing up. Masking tape or woodworking clamps work well to keep the backing fabric pulled taut. Try not to stretch the fabric.

Center the batting over the backing fabric. Use your hands to press any wrinkles out of the batting. Work from the center out toward the edges so that any excess batting gets pushed beyond the edge of backing.

When the batting is flat and free of wrinkles, center the quilt, right side up, over the backing and batting. Starting at the center and working outward, ease any wrinkles out of the top.

Pin or thread baste the quilt sandwich together, working from the center outward. For machine quilting, I prefer to pin baste with 1" brass safety pins, pinning every 6" to 8". When pinning, I try to anticipate where I'll be doing my straight-line quilting, and I avoid putting pins in that path. This allows me to quilt continuous lines without having to stop and remove safety pins.

Quilting

When making a quilt I plan to donate, I assume that the quilts are going to be used and washed regularly. That means that they need to be densely quilted.

When I begin to quilt, I first sew straight lines all the way across the quilt top. This stabilizes the entire top and provides the basis for all the quilting. I usually stitch these lines of anchor quilting between the blocks, in the sashing, or parallel to a major element of the block design.

Once the anchor quilting is complete, I may also do some free-motion quilting. Quilts with large open areas such as "Unequal Irish Chain" (page 88) and "Rainbow Lattice" (page 60) are excellent candidates for free-motion quilting.

Quilting designs and patterns are available from a variety of sources. Quilt books and magazines, as well as quilt stencils, offer a wide variety of quilting options. I've also gotten wonderful patterns from coloring books, cookie cutters, children's art stencils, and from motifs within fabric designs. Any simple outline shape can make a wonderful quilting pattern.

Free-motion quilting designs can be drawn directly on the quilt top before the quilt sandwich is assembled. Or, you can mark designs on tearaway quilt paper and then pin it where you want it on the quilt. You then sew on the line through the paper and the quilt. When you've completed the design, you then gently remove the paper. I prefer to use quilt paper.

I frequently don't make a decision about how to free-motion quilt a project until I see what it looks like after the initial straight-line anchor quilting is complete. Because it frees me from having to mark the quilt in advance, quilting paper allows me the flexibility to complete the straight-line quilting prior to making a decision on free-motion quilting.

Binding

The final stage of making your quilt is adding the binding. In order to do this, you must first trim off the excess batting and backing fabric.

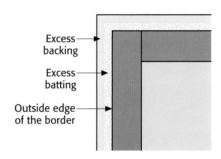

Excess backing
Excess batting
Outside edge of the border

Begin by measuring the width of the outermost border from the seam to the edge of the fabric. The border shoud be approximately ¼" larger than the desired finished size. For a quilt with a finished border size of 3", the unbound border should measure about 3¼".

Starting at the bottom edge of the quilt, line up the ruler line that is equal to the width of the border (3¼") with the inner seam of the border. The edge of the ruler should be about even with the outside edge of the quilt. Cut along the edge of the quilt, moving the ruler as needed.

To square the corners you'll need to line up the ruler line with both the side you just cut and the side you're going to cut.

Once you have the quilt sandwich trimmed, set it aside.

Making and Attaching the Binding Strip

Cut the required number of 2½"-wide binding strips for your project. Follow these steps to sew the strips together into one single binding strip.

To piece the binding strips:

1. Lay out the first binding strip right side up. Put a second binding strip, right sides together, on top of the end of the first strip at a 90° right angle. Make a diagonal line from the upper-left side to the lower-right side of the crossed binding strips; stitch. Repeat for any remaining strips.

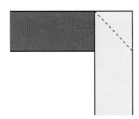

2. When the fabric strips are opened up, they should align at the edges and form a continuous line. Check that all the seams are sewn correctly and then trim the excess triangle pieces off approximately ¼" from the stitching lines.

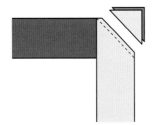

3. Lay out the binding strip so that the wrong side of the fabric is facing up. Fold the lower-left corner of the binding strip at a 90° angle so that it makes a triangle as shown.

4. Fold the binding strip in half the long way, wrong sides together, and press.

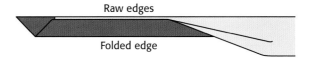

Raw edges

Folded edge

5. Start at a point midway along the side or bottom edge of your quilt. Do not begin at a corner. Align the raw edges of your binding strip with the edge of the quilt. Hold or pin the binding in place. Using a ¼" seam allowance, begin sewing about 4" from the end of the binding strip, sewing through the folded binding and quilt sandwich. Stitch slowly, keeping edges aligned. Stop sewing approximately ¼" from the corner.

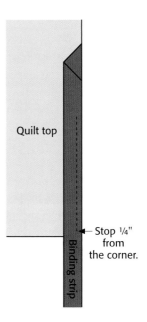

Quilt top

Binding strip

Stop ¼" from the corner.

6. Rotate your quilt 90° so that the side of the quilt with the binding is now at the top. Move the quilt out from under the needle and fold the binding up toward the sewn edge until it forms a 45° angle. Hold the fold in place with one hand, and fold the remainder of the binding strip back down so that there is a fold at

the top of the quilt and the raw edges of the binding line up with the side of the quilt. Using a ¼" seam allowance, sew through the folded edge of the binding from the top of the quilt. Continue down the side of the quilt.

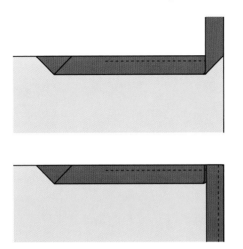

7. Fold and sew the remainder of the sides and corners in the same manner until you're approximately 6" from your starting point, and then stop sewing. Trim off excess binding approximately ½" beyond the starting point. Tuck the end of the binding into the fold and finish the seam.

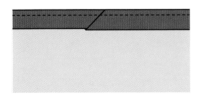

8. Working from the back of the quilt, fold the binding over the edge (from front to back) and pin in place. When pinning the binding, I pin parallel to the binding rather than across it. Pin several inches at a time.

Quilt back

9. Using a thread that blends with the binding fabric, blindstitch the binding to the back of the quilt. I generally sew four or five stitches per inch. At the corners, the binding should form a smooth 45° angle on the front and back of the quilt. Pin and sew the mitered corners in place.

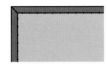

Labels

I make labels for all my quilts. The label is an important part of your quilt, so don't forget to add one. If the quilt is for me or for someone I know, I include the name of the quilt, the date I completed it, and my name and hometown. If it was made for a specific occasion, I note that on the label as well.

When you're making a quilt for donation, check to see if the recipient organization has rules about labels. They might even provide labels for you to use. For example, Project Linus gives quiltmakers satin labels to sew onto quilts. Each label features Linus from the *Peanuts* comic strip, with his blanket, and says, "Made With Tender Loving Care for Project Linus." If you choose to make and donate a quilt to Project Linus, the satin labels are available by contacting your local chapter.

Altering the Size of the Quilt

The quilts in this book are designed to be lap quilts. However, these patterns can easily be adapted to make larger or smaller quilts. Simply add or remove blocks.

Standard Quilt Dimensions

The following table shows typical quilt sizes for different bed sizes. These sizes can serve as a general guideline.

Twin	63" x 87"
Full	78" x 87"
Queen	84" x 92"
King	100" x 92"

Determining the Number of Blocks

To enlarge a quilt, refer back to the original pattern. The pattern information provides the finished block size as well as the sashing and border sizes.

- *Skill level:* beginner
- 20 blocks, 8" finished size
- 2" sashing
- 1" inner border
- 2½" outer border

To determine the number of blocks you'll need, subtract the width of the borders from the length and width of the desired quilt size. Divide the

remainder by the size of the finished quilt block. For example, to enlarge the "Block in a Box" quilt (page 29) to full size (approximately 78" x 87"), your calculation would look like this:

- 2" border x 2 = 4"
- 78" quilt width – 4" = 74" ÷ 6" block = 12 blocks
- 87" quilt length – 4" = 83" ÷ 6" block = 14 blocks

This quilt will have a 12 x 14 block layout for a total of 168 blocks. The finished dimensions will be 76" x 88":

- 12 blocks x 6" = 72" + 4" (borders) = 76"
- 14 blocks x 6" = 84" + 4" (borders) = 88"

If the pattern includes sashing strips, add the width of the sashing strip to the block size to determine the number of blocks needed. For example, the calculation for changing "Bordered Square" (page 32) into a full-size quilt (approximately 78" x 87") would look like this:

- 8" block plus 2" sashing = 10"
- 3½" borders x 2 = 7"
- 78" quilt width – 7" = 71" ÷ 10" = 7 blocks
- 87" quilt length – 7" = 80" ÷ 10" = 8 blocks

This quilt will have a 7 x 8 block layout for a total of 56 blocks. The finished dimensions will be 75" x 85":

- 7 blocks x 8" = 56" + 12" (sashing) + 7" (borders) = 75"
- 8 blocks x 8" = 64" + 14" (sashing) + 7" (borders) = 85"

Determining the Number of Pieces

The next step in altering the size of your quilt is to determine how many of each piece you'll need. You'll then use that information to determine how much fabric you should purchase.

Blocks

To determine how many of each piece you need, refer to the "Single Block Requirements" for your pattern. Multiply the number of pieces that you need to make one block by the number of blocks in your quilt. This will give you the number of pieces to cut for your quilt.

As an example, the single block requirements for the "Bordered Square" quilt are as follows:

- 12 bright squares, 2½" x 2½"
- 1 bright square, 4½" x 4½"

To enlarge this quilt to full size, you need 56 blocks. Multiply the number of each piece needed for a single block by 56 to get the total number needed. The calculation would look like this:

- 12 x 56 = 672 total 2½" bright squares
- 1 x 56 = 56 total 4½" bright squares

Sashing

Increasing the number of blocks means you'll also need to increase the number of sashing strips and sashing squares. Sashing strips go between the blocks, so there is one less sashing strip in each row than there are blocks in that row.

To determine the number of sashing strips needed, multiply the number of blocks by two, then subtract one sashing strip for each block along the right side and one sashing strip for each block along the bottom. For example, a full-size "Bordered Square" quilt would have 56 blocks in a 7 x 8 layout.

- 56 blocks x 2 = 112 − 7 = 105 − 8 = 97 sashing strips

The number of sashing *squares* in a quilt is determined by subtracting 1 from the number of blocks across and 1 from the number of blocks down and then multiplying the numbers. In a 7 x 8 block quilt, the sashing square layout would be 6 x 7, for a total of 42 sashing squares.

● ● ● ● ● ● Tip ● ● ● ● ● ●

If you're having a difficult time visualizing the blocks and sashing, draw a simple illustration.

Calculating Borders and Binding

When I calculate fabric requirements, I assume that the width of the fabric is 40" and no wider. Doing so will allow for fabric variations and shrinkage if you prewash your fabric. The number of border strips needed is determined by how many 40"-long strips it will take to reach your quilt's finished length and width. Divide the finished quilt size by 40 and round up to the nearest full or half strip.

For example, for a quilt that is 78" x 87", divide both 78" and 87" by 40, round up, and then double each amount because you'll need strips for the top and bottom, and for the left and right sides.

- 78 ÷ 40 = 1.95   round up to 2   2 x 2 = 4 border strips needed

- 87 ÷ 40 = 2.18   round up to 2.5   2.5 x 2 = 5 border strips needed

Add together the number needed for the sides and the number needed for the top and bottom of the quilt to determine the total number of strips to cut. This quilt needs a total of nine border strips cut the width of the fabric.

To determine the amount of binding needed, add the length and width of the quilt and multiply by 2, and then add 10" for seams and corners. Divide the result by 40 and round to the nearest whole number to determine the number of binding strips to cut. For a 78" x 87" quilt, you will need (78" + 87") x 2 = 330" +10" = 340" ÷ 40 = 8.5, which rounds up to 9 binding strips, 40" long. The number of binding strips required for your quilt is generally the same number of strips needed to make your largest border, but it is always a good idea to calculate the amount needed, to be certain.

Determining Fabric Requirements

Once you know the number of pieces of each color and size you need, you can figure out how much fabric to purchase.

First, divide the number of pieces needed in each size by the number of pieces of that size you can cut from a single fabric strip that is cut the width of the fabric. This will give you the number of strips that you need to cut. Round up to the nearest whole number.

Next, multiply the number of strips that you need by the width of the strips you need to cut. This gives you the exact number of inches of fabric you'll need. To calculate yardage, round up to the next full inch, and add 10% for a cushion in case of error. Round the final number up to the nearest eighth of a yard.

As an example, the block calculations for the full-size "Bordered Square" quilt would look like this:

Assorted bright fabrics:
- 714 squares, 2½" x 2½"
  (672 for blocks and 42 for sashing)
- Each 40" strip yields 16 squares.
- 714 ÷ 16 = 44.6 strips; round up to 45
- 45 x 2½" = 112½"

- 56 squares, 4½" x 4½" (blocks)
- Each 40" strip yields 8 squares.
- 56 ÷ 8 = 7 strips
- 7 x 4½" = 31½"

Add all the inches of the same fabric together, round up to the next full inch, and add 10% for a cushion in case of shrinkage or cutting error. To convert the result from inches to yards, divide the total by 36 and round up to the nearest eighth yard.

Using the numbers below left and above as an example:
- 112.5" + 31.5" = 144" x 0.10 = 14.4 + 144 = 158.4 ÷ 36 = 4.4; round up to 4.5 yards total of assorted bright fabrics

Repeat this step for each of the different fabrics used in the quilt. Rectangles are handled the same way as squares. Use the first dimension to determine the number of strips required; then multiply the number of strips by the second dimension. For example, calculate the amount of white fabric needed for the "Bordered Square" quilt:

- 97 rectangles, 2½" x 8½" (sashing strips)
- Each 40" strip yields 16 rectangles.
- 97 ÷ 16 = 6.1 strips; round up to 7
- 7 strips x 8½" = 59½"

- 9 strips, 1½" x 42" (inner border)
- 9 x 1½" = 13½"

- 59.5" + 13.5" = 73" x 0.10 = 7.3 + 73 = 80.3 ÷ 36 = 2.23; round up to 2.5 yards of white fabric

The handy charts below will make your calculations easier. The first chart indicates how many squares you can usually cut from a single strip of a particular width, assuming the strip measures at least 40" long. The second chart lists standard cuts of fabric along with their metric equivalents.

Strip Width	Piece Yield
1½"	26
2"	20
2½"	16
3"	13
3½"	11
4"	10
4½"	8
5"	8
5½"	7
6"	6
6½"	6
7"	5

Standard Cuts of Fabric	
⅛ yard = 4.5"	(.125 yard)
¼ yard = 9"	(.25 yard)
⅜ yard = 13.5"	(.375 yard)
½ yard = 18"	(.5 yard)
⅝ yard = 22.5"	(.625 yard)
¾ yard = 27"	(.75 yard)
⅞ yard = 31.5"	(.875 yard)
1 yard = 36"	(1.00 yard)
Fat quarter:	18" x 22"
Fat eighth:	9" x 22"

Arkansas Crossroads

45" x 57"

Made from 576 bright squares, this quilt provides a wonderful opportunity to use a wide variety of fabrics from your scrap bag.

Materials

Yardages are based on 42"-wide fabric.

2 yards *total* of assorted bright fabrics for blocks

1⅜ yards of cream fabric for blocks and inner border

⅝ yard of blue fabric for outer border

½ yard of lavender print for binding

3 yards of fabric for backing

49" x 61" piece of batting

Single Block Requirements

2 cream squares, 3½" x 3½"

12 assorted bright squares, 2" x 2"

Cutting

All measurements include ¼"-wide seam allowances.

From the assorted bright fabrics, cut:

● 576 squares, 2" x 2"

From the cream fabric, cut:

● 96 squares, 3½" x 3½"

● 5 strips, 2" x 42"

From the blue fabric, cut:

● 5 strips, 3½" x 42"

From the lavender print, cut:

● 6 strips, 2½" x 42"

Assembling the Blocks

1. Draw a diagonal line from corner to corner on the wrong side of 192 of the 2" bright squares. Align a 2" bright square with the upper-right corner of a 3½" cream square, right sides together. The drawn diagonal line should form a triangle at the corner as shown. Sew on the diagonal line. Trim the excess fabric ¼" from the sewn line. Press toward the bright corner.

Make 96.

2. Rotate the step 1 units 180°. As you did in step 1, sew a bright square to the upper-right corner of each unit to make 96 bright corner squares.

Bright corner square.
Make 96.

3. Sew the remaining 2" bright squares into 192 pairs. Press seam allowances to the left.

Make 192.

4. Divide the units into two groups and arrange so that in one group the seam allowances point to the left and in the other group the seam allowances point to the right. Pin and sew the units into four-patch units. Press.

Four-patch unit.
Make 96.

5. Pin and sew the four-patch units and the bright corner squares from step 2 into pairs. Press seam allowances toward the four-patch units.

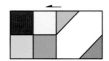

Make 96.

6. Divide the pairs into two groups and arrange so that in one group the four-patch units are on the left and in the other group the four-patch units are on the right. Pin and sew the pairs into 48 blocks. Press.

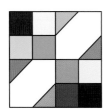

Completed block.
Make 48.

Assembling and Finishing the Quilt Top

1. Pin and sew the completed blocks into 24 pairs. Align the blocks so that the cream strips form a point. Press.

Make 24.

2. Arrange the pairs into blocks as shown, rotating one pair so that the cream fabric forms a diamond in the completed block. Pin and sew the pairs together, matching the center seams, to make 12 large blocks.

Make 12.

3. Arrange the 12 large blocks as shown. Sew the blocks into horizontal rows and join the rows.

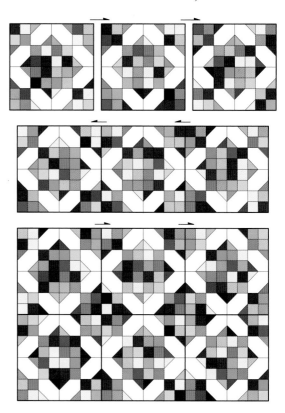

4. Referring to "Straight-Cut Borders" on page 17, measure, cut, and sew the 2" cream inner-border strips to the top and bottom edges of the quilt top first, and then to the side edges. Repeat with the 3½" blue outer-border strips.

5. Assemble the quilt sandwich as indicated in "Quiltmaking Basics" (page 18). Quilt as desired. Bind the edges using the lavender strips; add a label.

Block in a Box

40" x 52"

*Different shades of your favorite color can be brought
together and showcased in this quilt.*

Materials

Yardages are based on 42"-wide fabric.

2⅜ yards *total* of assorted purple fabrics for blocks, border corners, and binding

½ yard of blue fabric for border

⅜ yard *total* of assorted bright fabrics for blocks

2¾ yards of backing fabric*

44" x 56" piece of batting

If the backing fabric is wide enough after prewashing, it might be possible to use a single width of fabric, 1⅝ yards long.

Single Block Requirements

2 purple squares, 2½" x 2½"

1 bright square, 2½" x 2½"

2 purple rectangles, 2½" x 6½"

Cutting

All measurements include ¼"-wide seam allowances.

From the assorted purple fabrics, cut:

- 100 squares, 2½" x 2½"
- 96 rectangles, 2½" x 6½"
- 5 strips, 2½" x 42"

From the assorted bright fabrics, cut:

- 48 squares, 2½" x 2½"

From the blue fabric, cut:

- 5 strips, 2½" x 42"

Assembling the Blocks

1. Sew a purple square to opposite sides of a bright square as shown to make 48 center units. Press toward the purple squares.

Center unit.
Make 48.

2. Pin and sew 2½" x 6½" purple rectangles to each side of the center units as shown. Press toward the purple rectangles. Make 48.

Completed block.
Make 48.

Assembling and Finishing the Quilt Top

1. Divide the completed blocks into two groups. Align the blocks so that in one group the purple rectangles run horizontally, and in the other group they run vertically. Pin and sew the blocks into pairs. Press toward the block with the vertical rectangles.

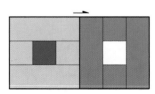

Make 24.

2. Divide the block pairs into two groups of 12 each. Align the block pairs so that in one group the horizontal rectangles are on the left, and in the other group the horizontal rectangles are on the right. Pin and sew the pairs together, matching the center seams, to make 12 large blocks. Press.

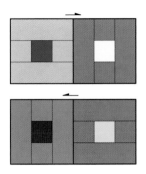 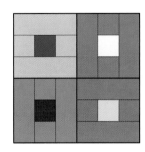

Make 12.

3. Sew the blocks into rows as shown and join the rows.

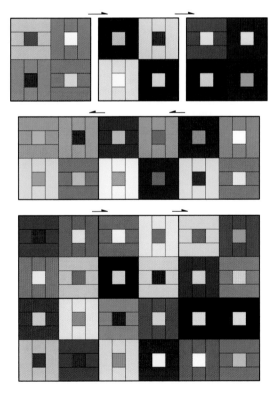

4. Referring to "Borders with Corner Squares" on page 18, measure and trim the 2½" blue border strips to the determined length, piecing as necessary. Sew the side border strips to the side edges of the quilt top. Sew a purple corner square to each end of the top and bottom border strips, and then sew the border strips to the top and bottom edges of the quilt top.

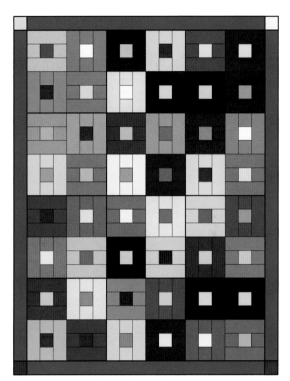

5. Assemble the quilt sandwich as indicated in "Quiltmaking Basics" (page 18). Quilt as desired. Bind the edges using the purple strips; add a label.

Bordered Square

45" x 55"

The 4½" center blocks in this quilt are perfect for large-scale novelty prints. If you decide to use a novelty fabric for this quilt, be sure to read "Fussy Cutting" on page 12.

- *Skill level:* beginner •
- 20 blocks, 8" finished size •
- 2" sashing •
- 1" inner border •
- 2½" outer border •

Materials

Yardages are based on 42"-wide fabric.

1¾ yards *total* of assorted bright fabrics for blocks*

1⅛ yards of white fabric for sashing and inner border

½ yard of red fabric for outer border

½ yard of purple fabric for binding

2¾ yards of fabric for backing

49" x 59" piece of batting

The fabric requirement listed here is for straight-cut fabric. If you want to fussy cut the center squares, as shown, see "Fussy Cutting" on page 12. You may need to purchase additional fabric.

Single Block Requirements

12 bright squares, 2½" x 2½"

1 bright square, 4½" x 4½"

Cutting

All measurements include ¼"-wide seam allowances.

From the assorted bright fabrics, cut:

- 252 squares, 2½" x 2½" *360 for bigger quilt*
- 20 squares, 4½" x 4½" *30*

From the white fabric, cut:

- 31 rectangles, 2½" x 8½"
- 5 strips, 1½" x 42"

From the red fabric, cut:

- 5 strips, 3" x 42"

From the purple fabric, cut:

- 6 strips, 2½" x 42"

Assembling the Blocks

1. Set aside 12 bright 2½" squares for the sashing. Sew the remaining 2½" bright squares into 120 pairs. Press the seams to one side.

Make 120.

2. Sew a pair of bright squares from step 1 to each side of the 4½" bright squares. Press toward the large squares. Make 20.

Make 20.

3. Sew the remaining pairs of bright squares into pairs to make 40 four-square units as shown. Press.

Make 40.

4. Pin and sew a four-square unit from step 3 to the top and bottom of each unit created in step 2. Press.

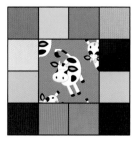

Completed block.
Make 20.

Assembling and Finishing the Quilt Top

1. Pin and sew 2½" x 8½" white sashing strips to the right side of 15 of the completed blocks and to the bottom of 4 of the completed blocks. Press toward the sashing strips.

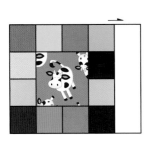

Make 15.

Make 4.

• • • • • • • • • **Tip** • • • • • • • • •

If you're using directional fabric in your quilt, make sure that all your blocks are oriented correctly before you begin adding sashing strips.

2. Sew 2½" bright sashing squares to one end of the 12 remaining 2½" x 8½" white sashing strips. Press toward the sashing strips.

Make 12.

3. Pin and sew the 12 sashing strips with squares to the bottoms of 12 of the blocks with side sashing. Press.

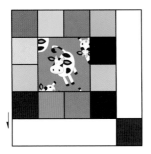

Make 12.

4. Arrange the block units as shown. Sew the units into horizontal rows and join the rows.

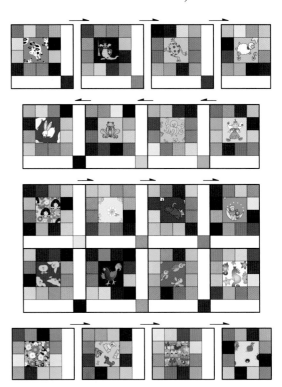

5. Referring to "Straight-Cut Borders" on page 17, measure, trim, and sew the 1½" white inner-border strips first to the top and bottom edges of the quilt and then to the side edges. Repeat with the 3" red outer-border strips.

6. Assemble the quilt sandwich as indicated in "Quiltmaking Basics" (page 18). Quilt as desired. Bind the edges using the purple strips; add a label.

Bright Hopes

43" x 55"

The Bright Hopes block only looks complex; it's actually relatively simple to construct. The off-center layout of the rectangles provides a great deal of movement within the quilt top.

Materials

Yardages are based on 42"-wide fabric.

1⅞ yards *total* of assorted bright fabrics for blocks

⅝ yard of white fabric for blocks and inner border

½ yard of blue fabric for outer border

½ yard of green fabric for binding

2⅞ yards of fabric for backing

47" x 59" piece of batting

Single Block Requirements

1 white square, 2½" x 2½"

4 bright rectangles, 2½" x 4½"

Cutting

All measurements include ¼"-wide seam allowances.

From the assorted bright fabrics, cut:

- 192 rectangles, 2½" x 4½"

From the white fabric, cut:

- 48 squares, 2½" x 2½"
- 5 strips, 1½" x 42"

From the blue fabric, cut:

- 5 strips, 3" x 42"

From the green fabric, cut:

- 6 strips, 2½" x 42"

Assembling the Blocks

1. Aligning the edges and keeping right sides together, place a white square at one end of a bright rectangle. Sew the pair together along the right side, ending approximately ½" from the bottom-right corner of the white square. The remaining part of the bright rectangle will hang loose.

2. *Finger-press* the seam toward the bright rectangle. Turn the unit a quarter turn to the *right* so that the center square is below the bright rectangle. Align a 2½" x 4½" bright rectangle with the right side of the unit. Sew, and press toward the bright rectangle.

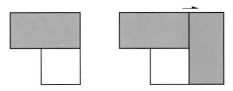

3. Rotate the block a quarter turn to the *left*. Sew a 2½" x 4½" bright rectangle to the right side of the unit from step 2. Press toward the bright rectangle just added.

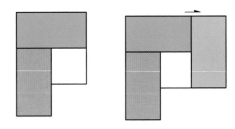

4. Rotate the block a quarter turn to the *left*. Fold the loose flap of the first bright rectangle back over itself and pin out of the way. Align a bright 2½" x 4½" rectangle with the right side of the

unit. Sew and press toward the bright rectangle just added.

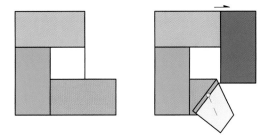

5. Rotate the block a quarter turn to the *left* so that the pinned rectangle is on the right side. Unpin the rectangle and finish sewing it to the block, overlapping a few stitches where it was previously sewn. Press toward the bright rectangle you just completed sewing to the block. Repeat the process to make 48 blocks.

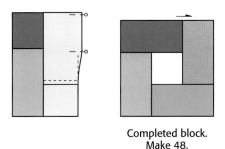

Completed block.
Make 48.

Assembling and Finishing the Quilt Top

1. Sew pairs of completed blocks together. Press toward the left.

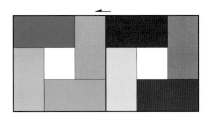

Make 24.

2. Divide the block pairs into two groups. Turn one group so that the center seam is pressed to the right, and the other group so that the center seam is pressed to the left. Pin and sew pairs together, matching the center seams, to make 12 large blocks. Press.

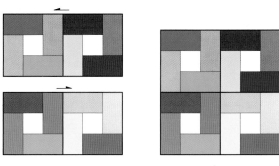

Make 12.

3. Arrange the 12 large blocks as shown. Sew the blocks into horizontal rows and join the rows.

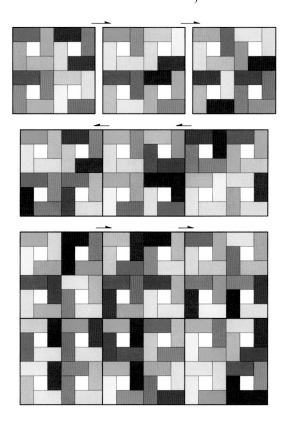

4. Referring to "Straight-Cut Borders" on page 17, measure, trim, and sew the 1½" white inner-border strips first to the top and bottom edges of the quilt and then to the side edges. Repeat with the 3" blue outer-border strips.

5. Assemble the quilt sandwich as indicated in "Quiltmaking Basics" (page 18). Quilt as desired. Bind the edges using the green strips; add a label.

Center Squares

42½" x 54½"

The large center blocks lend themselves beautifully to novelty fabrics. You can use several different novelties, or use a single center fabric and then select colors for the smaller squares that match the novelty fabric.

- **_Skill level:_** beginner •
- 12 blocks, 10½" finished size •
- 1½" sashing •
- 1½" inner border •
- 2½" outer border •

Materials

Yardages are based on 42"-wide fabric.

1½ yards of cream fabric for blocks, sashing and inner border

1 yard of purple fabric for blocks and outer border

½ yard of cat fabric for block centers and sashing squares*

½ yard _total_ of assorted bright fabrics OR ⅛ yard _each_ of 8 different bright fabrics for blocks

½ yard of blue fabric for binding

2⅞ yards of fabric for backing

47" x 59" piece of batting

*_The fabric requirement listed here is for straight-cut fabric. If you want to fussy cut your block centers, see "Fussy Cutting" on page 12. You may need to purchase double this amount of fabric or more._

Single Block Requirements

4 cream rectangles, 2" x 5"

4 purple rectangles, 2" x 5"

1 cat square, 5" x 5"

8 bright squares, 2" x 2"

8 cream squares, 2" x 2"

Cutting

All measurements include ¼"-wide seam allowances.

From the purple fabric, cut:

- 48 rectangles, 2" x 5"
- 5 strips, 3" x 42"

From the cream fabric, cut:

- 48 rectangles, 2" x 5"
- 96 squares, 2" x 2"
- 17 strips, 2" x 11"
- 5 strips, 2" x 42"

From the cat fabric, cut:

- 12 squares, 5" x 5"
- 6 squares, 2" x 2"

From the assorted bright fabrics, cut:

- 96 squares, 2" x 2" OR 12 squares, 2" x 2", from _each_ of the ⅛-yard cuts

From the blue fabric, cut:

- 6 strips, 2½" x 42"

Assembling the Blocks

1. Sew the 2" x 5" purple and cream rectangles into 48 pairs. Press toward the purple rectangles.

Make 48.

2. Pin and sew purple and cream pairs to opposite sides of each 5" cat square, as shown, to make 12 center units. Press toward the purple and cream pairs; set aside.

Center unit.
Make 12.

3. Sew the 2" cream squares and 2" bright squares into 96 pairs. Press toward the bright squares.

Make 96.

Tip

If you're using only eight fabrics for the bright squares (as opposed to random scraps from your collection), now is the time to determine how you want them paired up. Sort them with like fabrics together, and determine which fabrics you want to pair together prior to step 4.

4. Divide the pairs into two groups. Lay them out so that in one group the bright squares are on the left, and in the other group the bright squares are on the right. Pin pairs of units together, matching seams, and sew into four-patch squares. Press.

Four-patch square.
Make 48.

5. Pin and sew the completed four-patch squares to the ends of the remaining purple and cream rectangle units as shown, matching seams, to make the top and bottom units of the block. Press toward the rectangle unit.

Top/bottom unit.
Make 24.

6. Pin and sew the top and bottom units to the center unit as shown. Press.

Completed block.
Make 12.

Assembling and Finishing the Quilt Top

1. Pin and sew a 2" x 11" cream sashing strip to the right side of eight of the completed blocks and to the bottom edge of three of the completed blocks. Press toward the sashing.

Make 8.

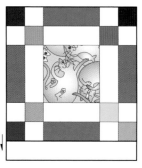

Make 3.

2. Sew a 2" cat sashing square to a 2" x 11" cream sashing strip. Press toward the sashing strip.

Make 6.

3. Pin and sew the sashing strips with squares to the bottom of six of the blocks with side sashing. Press toward the bottom sashing strips.

Make 6.

4. Arrange the block units as shown. Sew the units into horizontal rows and join the rows.

5. Referring to "Straight-Cut Borders" on page 17, measure, trim, and sew the 2" cream inner-border strip first to the top and bottom edges of the quilt top and then to the side edges. Repeat with the 3" purple outer-border strips.

6. Assemble the quilt sandwich as indicated in "Quiltmaking Basics" (page 18). Quilt as desired. Bind the edges using the blue strips; add a label.

Churn Dash

40" x 47"

*The Churn Dash block is a traditional favorite. Small-scale
novelty fabrics work very well in this block.*

Skill level: advanced beginner •

• 30 blocks, 6" finished size •

• 1" sashing •

• 1" inner border •

• 2" outer border •

Materials

Yardages are based on 42"-wide fabric.

1⅞ yards of white fabric for blocks, sashing, and inner border

1⅛ yards *total* of assorted bright fabrics for blocks

½ yard of purple fabric for sashing squares and binding

½ yard of blue fabric for outer border

2¾ yards of fabric for backing

44" x 51" piece of batting

Single Block Requirements

2 white squares, 3½" x 3½"

2 bright squares, 3½" x 3½"

4 white rectangles, 1½" x 2½"

4 bright rectangles, 1½" x 2½"

1 white square, 2½" x 2½"

Cutting

All measurements include ¼"-wide seam allowances.

From the white fabric, cut:

- 60 squares, 3½" x 3½"
- 120 rectangles, 1½" x 2½"
- 30 squares, 2½" x 2½"
- 49 strips, 1½" x 6½"
- 5 strips, 1½" x 42"

From the assorted bright fabrics, cut:

- 60 squares, 3½" x 3½"
- 120 rectangles, 1½" x 2½"

From the purple fabric, cut:

- 20 squares, 1½" x 1½"
- 5 strips, 2½" x 42"

From the blue fabric, cut:

- 5 strips, 2½" x 42"

Assembling the Blocks

1. Using the 3½" white squares and bright squares, assemble 120 half-square-triangle units (see "Half-Square-Triangle Units," page 14). Trim the units to 2½".

Make 120.

2. Sew the 1½" x 2½" white and bright rectangles into pairs as shown. Press toward the bright fabric.

3. Sew a rectangle unit from step 2 to one side of the 2½" white squares, with the bright rectangles adjoining the white squares. Press toward the bright rectangles. Repeat on the opposite side of the white squares to make 30 center units.

   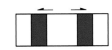

Center unit.
Make 30.

4. Sew a half-square-triangle unit to one side of the remaining rectangle units. Press toward the rectangle units. Repeat on the opposite side of each unit to make 60 top and bottom units.

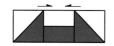

Top/bottom unit.
Make 60.

5. Pin and sew the top and bottom units to the center units as shown. Press.

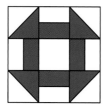

Completed block.
Make 30.

Assembling and Finishing the Quilt Top

1. Pin and sew 1½" x 6½" white sashing strips to the right side of all but one of the completed blocks. Press toward the sashing.

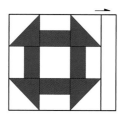

Make 29.

2. Sew the 1½" purple sashing squares to the end of the remaining 1½" x 6½" sashing strips. Press toward the sashing strips.

Make 20.

3. Pin and sew the sashing strips with squares to the bottom of 20 of the blocks with sashing. Press toward the sashing.

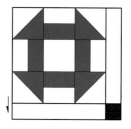

Make 20.

4. Pin and sew the blocks from step 3 into pairs as shown. Press.

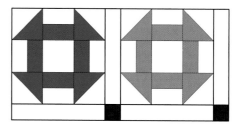

Make 10.

5. Pin and sew the units from step 4 into pairs to make a four-block unit as shown. There will be two units from step 4 remaining. Press.

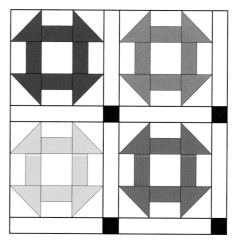

Make 4.

6. Pin and sew four of the remaining blocks with only *side* sashing into pairs. Press.

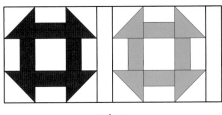

Make 2.

7. Pin and sew the two units from step 6 to the two remaining units from step 4. Press.

Make 2.

8. Pin and sew four of the blocks with sashing into pairs as shown. Sew the remaining block with sashing to the one block with no sashing. Press.

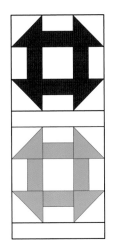 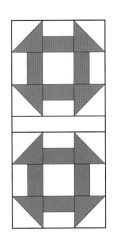

Make 2.   Make 1.

9. Arrange the units as shown. Sew the units into three horizontal sections and join the sections.

10. Referring to "Straight-Cut Borders" on page 17, measure, trim, and sew the 1½" white border strips first to the top and bottom edges of the quilt top and then to the side edges. Repeat with the 2½" blue outer-border strips.

11. Assemble the quilt sandwich as indicated in "Quiltmaking Basics" (page 18). Quilt as desired. Bind the edges using the purple strips; add a label.

Farmer's Flowers

41" x 52½"

The light blue fabric sets the tone for this entire quilt. The light blue squares and border add a calm counterpoint to the bright points and centers. A more intense blue would give those same points and centers a very different feel.

- **Skill level:** advanced beginner •
- 12 blocks, 10" finished size •
  - 1½" sashing •
  - 1½" inner border •
  - 2½" outer border •

Materials

Yardages are based on 42"-wide fabric.

2⅛ yards of cream fabric for blocks, sashing, and inner border

⅞ yard of light blue fabric for blocks, sashing squares, and outer border

⅝ yard *total* of assorted bright fabrics for blocks*

½ yard of lavender fabric for binding

2¾ yards of fabric for backing**

45" x 56½" piece of batting

The fabric requirement listed here is for straight-cut fabric. If you want to fussy cut the center squares as shown, see "Fussy Cutting" on page 12. You may need to purchase additional fabric.

**If the backing fabric is wide enough after prewashing, it might be possible to use a single width of fabric, 1⅝ yards long.*

Single Block Requirements

4 bright squares, 3½" x 3½"

4 cream squares, 3½" x 3½"

4 light blue squares, 2½" x 2½"

4 cream squares, 2½" x 2½"

4 cream rectangles, 2½" x 4½"

1 bright square, 2½" x 2½"

Cutting

All measurements include ¼"-wide seam allowances.

From the cream fabric, cut:

- 48 squares, 3½" x 3½"
- 48 squares, 2½" x 2½"
- 48 rectangles, 2½" x 4½"
- 17 rectangles, 2" x 10½"
- 5 strips, 2" x 42"

From the assorted bright fabrics, cut:

- 48 squares, 3½" x 3½"
- 12 squares, 2½" x 2½"

From the light blue fabric, cut:

- 48 squares, 2½" x 2½"
- 6 squares, 2" x 2"
- 5 strips, 3" x 42"

From the lavender fabric, cut:

- 6 strips, 2½" x 42"

Assembling the Blocks

1. Using the 3½" cream squares and bright squares, assemble 96 half-square-triangle units (see "Half-Square-Triangle Units," page 14). Trim to 2½".

Make 96.

2. Sew a half-square-triangle unit to each 2½" light blue square, aligning as shown. Press toward the blue squares. Make 48.

Make 48.

3. In the same manner sew the remaining half-square-triangle units to the 2½" cream squares. Press toward the cream squares.

Make 48.

4. Pin and sew the units from steps 3 and 4 together, matching center seams, to make 48 petal units. The solid squares should be opposite each other, and the points of the triangles should touch. Press.

Petal unit.
Make 48.

5. Pin and sew a completed petal unit to a long side of a 2½" x 4½" cream rectangle. Press toward the cream rectangle. Repeat on the opposite side of the cream rectangles to make 24 top and bottom units.

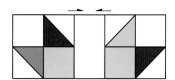

Top/bottom unit.
Make 24.

6. Sew a remaining 2½" x 4½" cream rectangle to one side of the 2½" bright squares. Press toward the cream rectangles. Repeat on the opposite side of the bright squares to make 12 center units.

Center unit.
Make 12.

7. Pin and sew the top and bottom units to the center units. Press.

Completed block.
Make 12.

Assembling and Finishing the Quilt Top

1. Pin and sew 2" x 10½" cream sashing strips to the right side of eight of the completed blocks and to the bottom of three of the completed blocks. Press toward the sashing strips.

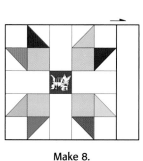 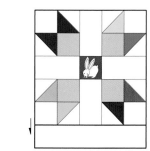

Make 8.   Make 3.

2. Sew 2" light blue sashing squares to the remaining cream sashing strips. Press toward the sashing strips.

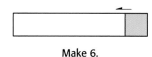

Make 6.

3. Pin and sew the sashing strips with squares to the bottoms of six of the blocks with side sashing. Press.

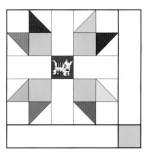

Make 6.

4. Arrange the block units as shown. Sew the units into horizontal rows and join the rows .

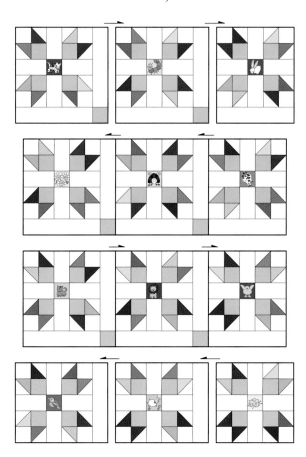

5. Referring to "Straight-Cut Borders" on page 17, measure, trim, and sew the 2" cream border strips first to the top and bottom edges of the quilt top and then to the side edges. Repeat with the 3" light blue outer-border strips.

6. Assemble the quilt sandwich as indicated in "Quiltmaking Basics" (page 18). Quilt as desired. Bind the edges using the lavender strips; add a label.

Greek Cross

46" x 61"

*Using a variety of values within the same color family for
each Greek Cross block provides a tremendous amount of visual interest.*

Materials

Yardages are based on 42"-wide fabric.

2⅜ yards *total* of assorted bright fabrics for blocks and binding

2 yards of assorted cream and white fabrics for blocks and inner border

¾ yard of blue fabric for outer border

2⅝ yards of fabric for backing

50" x 65" piece of batting

Single Block Requirements

2 cream/white squares, 4" x 4"

2 bright squares, 4" x 4"

4 cream/white rectangles, 1¾" x 3"

4 bright rectangles, 1¾" x 3"

1 bright square, 3" x 3"

Cutting

All measurements include ¼"-wide seam allowances.

From the assorted cream and white fabrics, cut:

- 70 squares, 4" x 4"
- 140 rectangles, 1¾" x 3"
- 5 strips, 1¾" x 42"

From the assorted bright fabrics, cut:

- 70 squares, 4" x 4"
- 140 rectangles, 1¾" x 3"
- 35 squares, 3" x 3"
- 6 strips, 2½" x 42"

From the blue fabric, cut:

- 6 strips, 3½" x 42"

Assembling the Blocks

1. Using the 4" cream/white squares and bright squares, assemble 140 half-square-triangle units (see "Half-Square-Triangle Units," page 14). Trim the squares to 3".

Make 140.

2. Sew the 1¾" x 3" cream/white rectangles and bright rectangles into 140 pairs along their long sides. Press toward the bright fabric.

Make 140.

3. Sew a rectangle unit from step 2 to one side of each 3" bright square, with the cream/white rectangles adjoining the bright squares. Press toward the bright squares. Repeat on the opposite side of the bright squares.

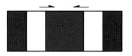

Center unit.
Make 35.

4. Sew a half-square-triangle unit to one side of the remaining rectangle units. Press toward the half-square-triangle units. Repeat on the opposite side of the rectangle units, as shown, to make top and bottom units.

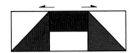

Top/bottom unit.
Make 70.

5. Pin and sew the top and bottom units from step 4 to the center units from step 3. Press.

Completed block.
Make 35.

Assembling and Finishing the Quilt Top

1. Pin and sew the completed blocks into 17 pairs. Press. There will be one block remaining.

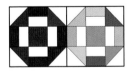

Make 17.

2. Pin and sew 12 of the units from step 1 into pairs to make six four-block units. Press.

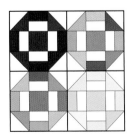

Make 6.

3. Arrange the block units as shown. Sew into horizontal sections and join the sections.

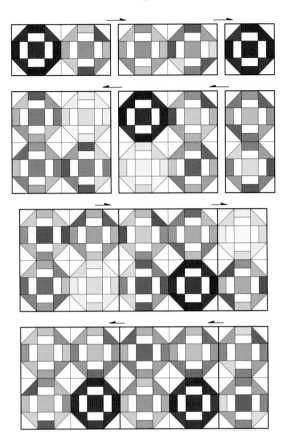

4. Referring to "Straight-Cut Borders" on page 17, measure, trim, and sew the 1¾" cream/white border strips first to the top and bottom edges of the quilt top and then to the side edges. Repeat with the 3½" blue outer-border strips.

5. Assemble the quilt sandwich as indicated in "Quiltmaking Basics" (page 18). Quilt as desired. Bind the edges using the bright strips; add a label.

Hen and Her Chicks

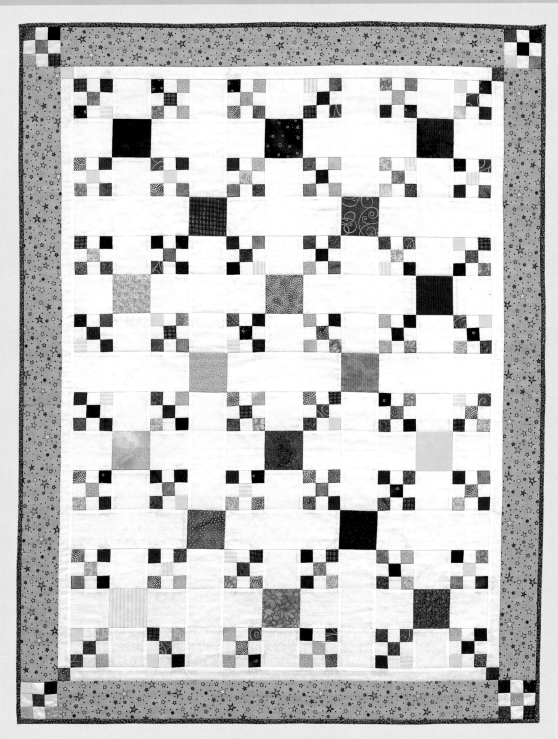

41" x 53"

The pieced border corners add whimsy to the finished quilt and provide continuity from the quilt center to the borders. This type of pieced border can be added to any quilt to increase visual interest.

- *Skill level:* intermediate ●
- 12 blocks, 9" finished size ●
- 3" sashing ●
- 1" inner border ●
- 3" outer border ●

Materials

Yardages are based on 42"-wide fabric.

1⅝ yards of white fabric for blocks, sashing strips, and border

¾ yard *total* of assorted bright fabrics for blocks, sashing squares, and border corner squares

⅝ yard of green fabric for outer border

½ yard of purple fabric for binding

2¾ yards of fabric for backing

45" x 57" piece of batting

Single Block Requirements

16 white squares, 1½" x 1½"

20 bright squares, 1½" x 1½"

4 white squares, 3½" x 3½"

1 bright square, 3½" x 3½"

Cutting

All measurements include ¼"-wide seam allowances.

From the white fabric, cut:

- 208 squares, 1½" x 1½"
- 48 squares, 3½" x 3½"
- 17 rectangles, 3½" x 9½"
- 5 strips, 1½" x 42"

From the assorted bright fabrics, cut:

- 264 squares, 1½" x 1½"
- 18 squares, 3½" x 3½"

From the green fabric, cut:

- 5 strips, 3½" x 42"

From the purple fabric, cut:

- 5 strips, 2½" x 42"

Assembling the Blocks

1. Set aside four 1½" bright squares for the inner border. Sew 1½" bright squares to opposite sides of 104 white 1½" squares. Press toward the bright squares.

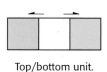

Top/bottom unit.
Make 104.

2. Sew 1½" white squares to opposite sides of the remaining 1½" bright squares to make 52 center units. Press toward the bright fabric.

Center unit.
Make 52.

3. Pin and sew the top and bottom units to opposite sides of the center units. Press. Set aside four nine-patch units for use in the border.

Nine-patch unit.
Make 52.

4. Pin and sew nine-patch units to opposite sides of 24 white 3½" squares. Press toward the white square.

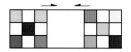

Top/bottom unit.
Make 24.

5. Sew 3½" white squares to opposite sides of 3½" bright squares to make center units. Make 12. Press toward the white squares.

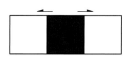

Center unit.
Make 12.

6. Pin and sew the top and bottom units to opposite sides of the center units to make nine-patch blocks. Press toward the center units.

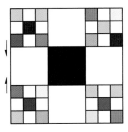

Completed block.
Make 12.

7. Pin and sew 3½" x 9½" white sashing strips to the right side of 11 of the completed blocks. There will be 1 block without sashing. Press toward the sashing strips.

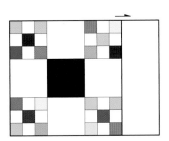

Make 11.

8. Sew 3½" bright squares to one end of six 3½" x 9½" white sashing strips. Press toward the sashing strips.

Make 6.

9. Pin and sew the sashing strips with squares to the bottoms of six of the blocks with side sashing. Press.

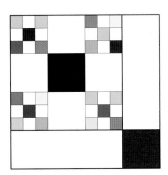

Make 6.

10. Arrange the block units as shown. Sew the blocks into horizontal rows and join the rows.

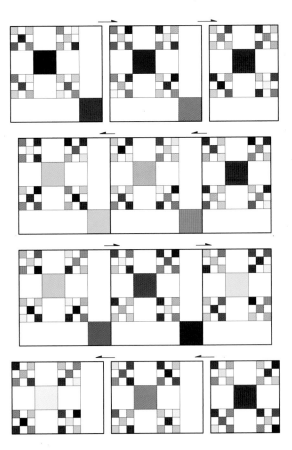

11. Referring to "Borders with Corner Squares" on page 18, measure and trim the 1½" white inner-border strips to the determined length, piecing as necessary. Sew the side-border strips to the side edges of the quilt top. Sew a 1½" bright square to each end of the top and bottom inner-border strips and then sew the border strips to the top and bottom edges of the quilt top.

12. Repeat step 11 for the 3½" green outer-border strips, using nine-patch units for the corner squares.

13. Assemble the quilt sandwich as indicated in "Quiltmaking Basics" (page 18). Quilt as desired. Bind the edges using the purple strips; add a label.

43½" x 55½"

Lincoln's Platform is an example of a structured scrap quilt. The dark blue fabric provides a focus and structure for the rest of the quilt.

Materials

Yardages are based on 42"-wide fabric.

2⅛ yards of white fabric for blocks, sashing, and inner border

1⅛ yards of blue fabric for blocks, sashing squares, and outer border

1 yard *total* of assorted bright fabrics for blocks and binding

3 yards of fabric for backing

48" x 60" piece of batting

Single Block Requirements

2 white squares, 4½" x 4½"

2 blue squares, 4½" x 4½"

8 white squares, 2" x 2"

12 bright squares, 2" x 2"

4 white rectangles, 2" x 5"

1 blue square, 2" x 2"

Cutting

All measurements include ¼"-wide seam allowances.

From the blue fabric, cut:

- 24 squares, 4½" x 4½"
- 18 squares, 2" x 2"
- 5 strips, 3½" x 42"

From the white fabric, cut:

- 24 squares, 4½" x 4½"
- 96 squares, 2" x 2"
- 48 rectangles, 2" x 5"
- 17 strips, 2" x 11"
- 5 strips, 2" x 42"

From the assorted bright fabrics, cut:

- 144 squares, 2" x 2"
- 6 strips, 2½" x 42"

Assembling the Blocks

1. Sew the 4½" blue squares and white squares together to form half-square-triangle units (see "Half-Square-Triangle Units," page 14). Trim to 3½".

Make 48.

2. Sew 2" white squares and bright squares together to make 96 pairs. Press toward the white squares.

Make 96.

3. Sew a unit from step 2 to each of the half-square-triangle units as shown. Press toward the white and bright pair.

Make 48.

4. Sew a 2" bright square to each of the remaining 48 units from step 2 as shown. Press toward the white fabric.

Make 48.

5. Pin a pieced strip from step 4 to each of the half-square-triangle units from step 3 as shown, matching seams. Sew and press toward the pieced strips just added.

Triangle unit.
Make 48.

6. Pin and sew 2" x 5" white rectangles to the right side of 24 of the triangle units. Press toward the white rectangle. Add another triangle unit to the opposite side of the white rectangles as shown.

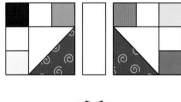

Top/bottom unit.
Make 24.

7. To make center units, sew 2" x 5" white rectangles to opposite sides of 12 of the 2" blue squares. Press toward the white rectangles.

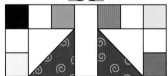

Center unit.
Make 12.

8. Pin and sew the top and bottom units to the center units. Press.

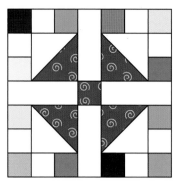

Completed block.
Make 12.

Assembling and Finishing the Quilt Top

1. Pin and sew 2" x 11" white sashing strips to the right side of 11 of the completed blocks. There will be 1 block with no sashing. Press toward the sashing strips.

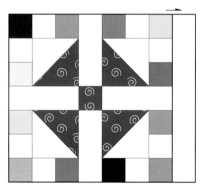

Make 11.

2. Sew the six remaining 2" blue squares to the remaining 2" x 11" white sashing strips. Press toward the sashing strips.

Make 6.

3. Pin and sew the sashing strips with squares to the bottoms of six of the blocks with side sashing. Press.

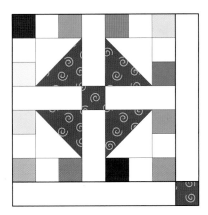

Make 6.

4. Arrange the block units as shown. Sew into horizontal rows and join the rows.

5. Referring to "Straight-Cut Borders" on page 17, measure, trim, and sew the 2" white inner-border strips first to the top and bottom edges of the quilt top and then to the side edges. Repeat with the 3½" blue outer-border strips.

6. Assemble the quilt sandwich as indicated in "Quiltmaking Basics" (page 18). Quilt as desired. Bind the edges using the bright strips; add a label.

Rainbow Lattice

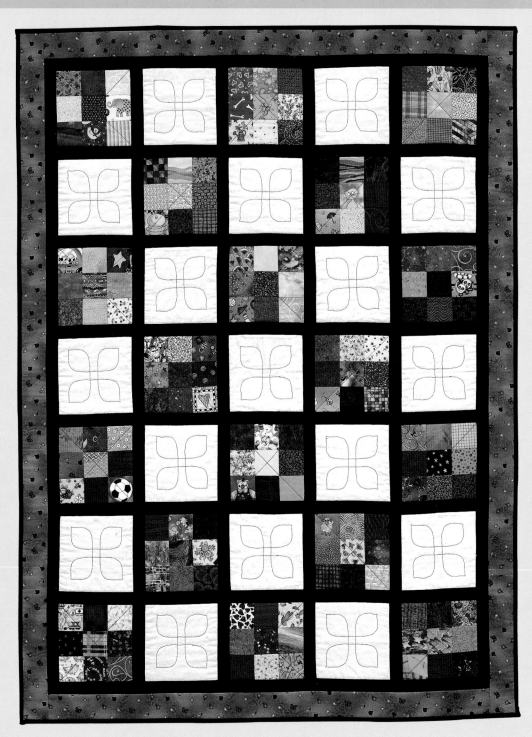

40" x 54"

The black sashing fabric provides an excellent contrast to the bright colors in this quilt. The large white blocks balance the colored blocks and are an excellent place for free-motion quilting.

• **_Skill level:_** beginner •

• 35 blocks, 6" finished size •

• 18 A blocks •

• 17 B blocks •

• 1" sashing •

• 2" outer border •

Materials

Yardages are based on 42"-wide fabric.

1⅜ yards of black fabric for inner sashing, outer sashing, and binding

⅞ yard _total_ of assorted bright fabrics for blocks

⅞ yard of white fabric for blocks

½ yard of blue fabric for border

2¾ yards of backing fabric*

44" x 58" piece of batting

*If the backing fabric is wide enough after prewashing, it might be possible to use a single width of fabric, 1⅞ yards long.

Single Block A Requirements

9 bright squares, 2½" x 2½"

Single Block B Requirements

1 white square, 6½" x 6½"

Cutting

All measurements include ¼"-wide seam allowances.

From the assorted bright fabrics, cut:

• 162 squares, 2½" x 2½"

From the white fabric, cut:

• 17 squares, 6½" x 6½"

From the black fabric, cut:

• 28 rectangles, 1½" x 6½"

• 11 strips, 1½" x 42"

• 5 strips, 2½" x 42"

From the blue fabric, cut:

• 5 strips, 2½" x 42"

Assembling the Blocks

1. Sew 2½" bright squares into 54 pairs. Press to the left. Sew another bright square to the end of each pair of bright squares. Press to the left.

Make 54.

2. Divide the pieced strips from step 1 into groups of three. Rotate each center strip so that the seam allowance points in the opposite direction of the top and bottom units. This will make it easier to match seams when pinning. Pin and sew the top and center strips together, matching seams. Press toward the center strip. Pin and sew the remaining strip to the bottom, matching seams, to complete the A blocks. Press toward the center strip.

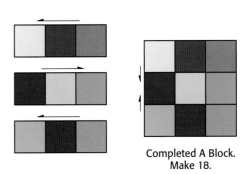

Completed A Block.
Make 18.

Assembling and Finishing the Quilt Top

1. Set aside four A blocks and three 6½" white B blocks.

2. Pin and sew 1½" x 6½" black sashing strips to the remaining A and B blocks. Press toward the sashing strips.

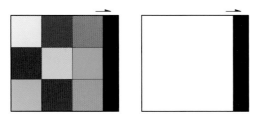

Make 14 of each.

3. Pin and sew the blocks from steps 1 and 2 into rows as shown, pressing toward the sashing strips.

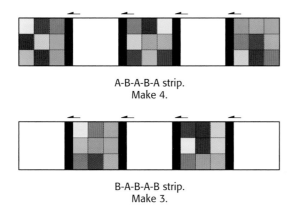

A-B-A-B-A strip.
Make 4.

B-A-B-A-B strip.
Make 3.

4. Sew 1½" black sashing strips to the bottom edges of all seven block strips. Trim off the excess fabric. Press.

5. Divide the block strips into A-B-A-B-A and B-A-B-A-B sets. Pin and sew A-B-A-B-A strips to the tops of the B-A-B-A-B strips as shown, carefully aligning the sashing strips. Press. You will have one A-B-A-B-A strip left over. Arrange the strips as shown above right and join the strips.

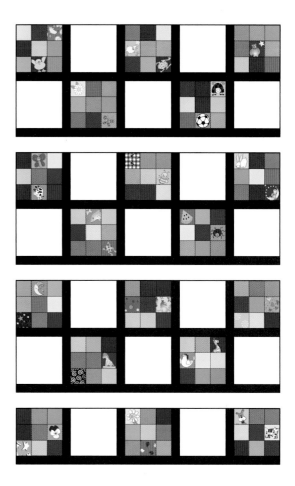

6. Sew a 1½" black sashing strip to the top edge of the quilt. Trim the strip even with the edges of the quilt top. Press toward the sashing.

7. Cut one of the remaining 1½" black sashing strips in half to form two pieces, approximately 20" long. Sew one piece to each of the remaining 1½" black sashing strips to create two long black sashing strips.

8. Sew the long black sashing strips to the sides of the quilt top. Press toward the sashing.

9. Referring to "Straight-Cut Borders" on page 17, measure, trim, and sew the 2½" blue border strips first to the top and bottom edges of the quilt top and then to the side edges.

10. Assemble the quilt sandwich as indicated in "Quiltmaking Basics" (page 18). Quilt as desired. Bind the edges using the black strips; add a label.

Shoo Fly

41" x 48"

The Shoo Fly, like the Churn Dash, is a traditional favorite. The feel of the quilt will be greatly influenced by the fabrics you select. Batiks would give it a contemporary quality, whereas floral or reproduction fabric would give it a vintage feel.

- **Skill level:** advanced beginner •
- 30 blocks, 6" finished size •
- 1" sashing •
- 1" inner border •
- 2¼" outer border •

Materials

Yardages are based on 42"-wide fabric.

1¾ yards of cream fabric for blocks and sashing

⅞ yard *total* of assorted bright fabrics for blocks and sashing squares

½ yard of fish print for outer border

¼ yard of pink fabric for inner border

½ yard of dark purple fabric for binding

2¾ yards of fabric for backing*

45" x 52" piece of batting

If the backing fabric is wide enough after prewashing, it might be possible to use a single width of fabric, 1⅝ yards long.

Single Block Requirements

2 cream squares, 3½" x 3½"

2 bright squares, 3½" x 3½"

4 cream squares, 2½" x 2½"

1 bright square, 2½" x 2½"

Cutting

All measurements include ¼"-wide seam allowances.

From the cream fabric, cut:

- 60 squares, 3½" x 3½"
- 120 squares, 2½" x 2½"
- 49 strips, 1½" x 6½"

From the assorted bright fabrics, cut:

- 60 squares, 3½" x 3½"
- 30 squares, 2½" x 2½"
- 20 squares, 1½" x 1½"

From the pink fabric, cut:

- 5 strips, 1½" x 42"

From the fish print, cut:

- 5 strips, 2¾" x 42"

From the dark purple fabric, cut:

- 5 strips, 2½" x 42"

Assembling the Blocks

1. Sew the 3½" cream squares and bright squares together to form 120 half-square-triangle units (see "Half-Square-Triangle Units," page 14). Trim squares to 2½".

Make 120.

2. Sew a 2½" cream square to one side of each 2½" bright square. Press toward the cream squares. Repeat on the opposite side of the bright squares to make 30 center units.

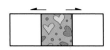

Center unit.
Make 30.

3. Sew a half-square-triangle unit to one side of each remaining 2½" cream square. Press toward the cream squares. Repeat on the opposite sides of the cream squares to make 60 top and bottom units as shown.

Top/bottom unit.
Make 60.

4. Pin and sew the top and bottom units to the center units as shown. Press toward the center units.

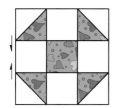

Completed block.
Make 30.

Assembling and Finishing the Quilt Top

1. Pin and sew 1½" x 6½" cream sashing strips to the right side of 29 of the completed blocks. There will be 1 block without a sashing strip. Press toward the sashing.

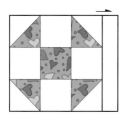

Make 29.

2. Sew a 1½" sashing square to one end of each of the remaining sashing strips. Press toward the sashing strips.

Make 20.

3. Pin and sew the sashing strips with squares to the bottoms of 20 of the blocks with side sashing. Press toward the sashing.

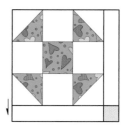

Make 20.

4. Pin and sew the blocks with side and bottom sashing into pairs. Press.

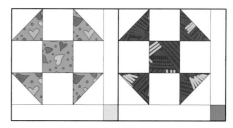

Make 10.

5. Pin and sew eight of the units from step 4 into pairs to make four-block units.

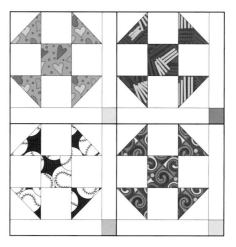

Four-block unit.
Make 4.

6. Pin and sew four of the remaining blocks with only *side* sashing into pairs. Press.

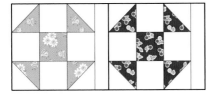

Make 2.

7. Pin and sew the two remaining units from step 4 to the units from step 6 as shown. Make 2.

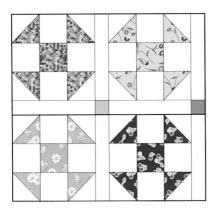

Four-block unit.
Make 2.

8. Pin and sew four of the blocks with sashing into pairs as shown. Sew the remaining block with sashing to the one block with no sashing. Press.

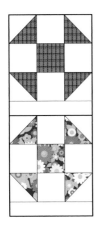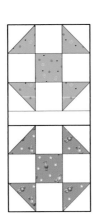

Make 2.   **Make 1.**

9. Arrange the block units as shown. Sew into horizontal sections. Join the sections.

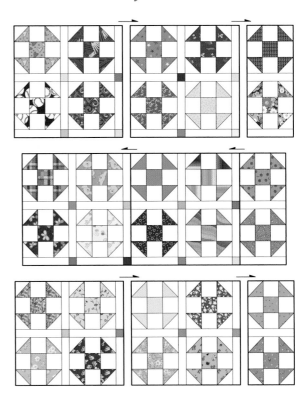

10. Referring to "Straight-Cut Borders" on page 17, measure, trim, and sew the 1½" pink inner-border strips first to the top and bottom edges of the quilt top and then to the side edges. Repeat with the 2¾" fish print outer-border strips.

11. Assemble the quilt sandwich as indicated in "Quiltmaking Basics" (page 18). Quilt as desired. Bind the edges using the dark purple strips; add a label.

Simple Nine Patch

44" x 60"

This simple block, with its structured colors, makes for a beautiful, relaxing quilt. To achieve a soft, harmonious look for your blocks, select coordinating colors with minimal contrast.

Materials

Yardages are based on 42"-wide fabric.

1⅜ yards of blue-and-purple batik for sashing and border

⅞ yard of light blue fabric for blocks

⅞ yard of dark blue fabric for blocks

⅝ yard of purple fabric for sashing squares and binding

¼ yard of green fabric for blocks

3 yards of fabric for backing

48" x 64" piece of batting

Single Block Requirements

1 green square, 2½" x 2½"

4 light blue squares, 2½" x 2½"

4 dark blue squares, 2½" x 2½"

Cutting

All measurements include ¼"-wide seam allowances.

From the light blue fabric, cut:

- 140 squares, 2½" x 2½"

From the green fabric cut:

- 35 squares, 2½" x 2½"

From the dark blue fabric, cut:

- 140 squares, 2½" x 2½"

From the blue and purple batik, cut:

- 58 rectangles, 2½" x 6½"
- 5 strips, 3½" x 42"

From the purple fabric, cut:

- 24 squares, 2½" x 2½"
- 6 strips, 2½" x 42"

Assembling the Blocks

1. Sew 2½" light blue and green squares into 35 units as shown. Press toward the blue squares.

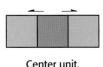

Center unit.
Make 35.

2. Sew 2½" dark blue squares to opposite sides of the remaining 2½" light blue squares. Press toward the light blue squares.

Top/bottom unit.
Make 70.

3. Pin and sew the top and bottom units to the center units, as shown, matching seams. Press toward the top and bottom units.

Completed block.
Make 35.

Assembling and Finishing the Quilt Top

1. Pin and sew 2½" x 6½" blue-and-purple batik sashing strips to the right side of all but one of the blocks. Press toward the sashing.

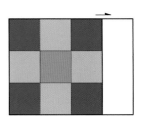

Make 34.

2. Sew 2½" purple sashing squares to one end of 24 of the 2½" x 6½" blue-and-purple batik sashing strips. Press toward the sashing strips.

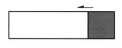

Make 24.

3. Pin and sew the sashing strips with squares to the bottoms of 24 of the blocks with side sashing. Press toward the bottom sashing strips.

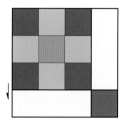

Make 24.

4. Pin and sew the blocks from step 3 into pairs. Press.

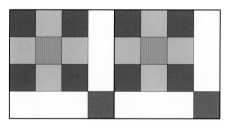

Make 12.

5. Pin and sew two block units from step 4 into pairs, as shown, to make four-block units. Press.

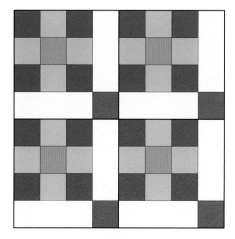

Four-block unit.
Make 6.

6. Sew the 10 blocks with only side sashing into pairs. Press.

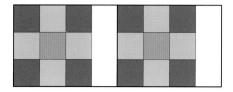

Make 5.

7. Arrange the units as shown. Sew into horizontal sections and join the sections.

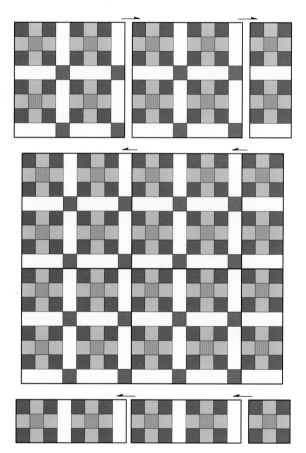

8. Referring to "Straight-Cut Borders" on page 17, measure, trim, and sew the 3½" blue-and-purple batik border strips first to the top and bottom edges of the quilt top and then to the side edges.

9. Assemble the quilt sandwich as indicated in "Quiltmaking Basics" (page 18). Quilt as desired. Bind the edges using the purple strips; add a label.

Single Chain and Knot

40" x 51½"

You can dramatically change the intensity of a quilt by adding or removing sashing strips. This open, airy quilt would feel very different if the sashing strips were removed to bring the four small squares at the corners of the blocks together.

Materials

Yardages are based on 42"-wide fabric.

2¼ yards of white fabric for blocks, sashing, inner border, and binding

⅞ yard of blue fabric for blocks, sashing squares, and outer border

⅜ yard *total* of assorted bright fabrics for blocks

2¾ yards of fabric for backing*

44" x 56" piece of batting

*If the backing fabric is wide enough after prewashing, it might be possible to use a single width of fabric, 1⅝ yards long.

Single Block Requirements

4 blue squares, 2½" x 2½"

4 white squares, 2½" x 2½"

1 bright square, 2½" x 2½"

8 bright squares, 1½" x 1½"

8 white squares, 1½" x 1½"

4 white rectangles, 2½" x 6½"

Cutting

All measurements include ¼"-wide seam allowances.

From the blue fabric, cut:

- 48 squares, 2½" x 2½"
- 6 squares, 2" x 2"
- 5 strips, 3" x 42"

From the white fabric, cut:

- 48 squares, 2½" x 2½"
- 96 squares, 1½" x 1½"
- 48 rectangles, 2½" x 6½"
- 17 strips, 2" x 10½"
- 5 strips, 1½" x 42"
- 5 strips, 2½" x 42"

From the assorted bright fabrics, cut:

- 12 squares, 2½" x 2½"
- 96 squares, 1½" x 1½"

Assembling the Blocks

1. Sew blue 2½" squares to 24 white 2½" squares. Press toward the blue squares. Repeat on the opposite side of the white squares to make top and bottom units as shown.

Top/bottom unit.
Make 24.

2. In the same manner, sew 24 white 2½" squares to opposite sides of 12 bright 2½" squares to make center units. Press toward the bright squares.

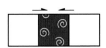

Center unit.
Make 12.

3. Pin and sew the top and bottom units to the center units, as shown, matching seams. Press toward the top and bottom units.

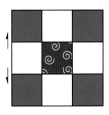

Nine-patch unit.
Make 12.

4. Pin and sew 2½" x 6½" white rectangles to opposite sides of the nine-patch units. Press toward the white rectangles. Set aside.

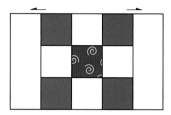

Make 12.

5. Sew the 1½" white squares and bright squares into 96 pairs. Press toward the bright squares.

Make 96.

6. Divide the pairs into two groups and arrange so that in one group the bright square is on the left, and in the other group the bright square is on the right. Pin, matching seams, and sew into four-patch units. Press.

Four-patch unit.
Make 48.

7. Pin and sew four-patch units to opposite sides of the remaining white 2½" x 6½" rectangles as shown. Press toward the rectangles.

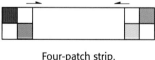

Four-patch strip.
Make 24.

8. Pin and sew the completed four-patch strips to the top and bottom of the units from step 4. The bright corners of the four-patch units should meet the blue corners of the nine-patch units as shown.

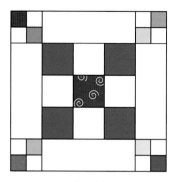

Completed block.
Make 12.

Assembling and Finishing the Quilt Top

1. Pin and sew 2" x 10½" white sashing strips to the right side of 11 of the completed blocks. There will be one block without sashing. Press toward the sashing strips.

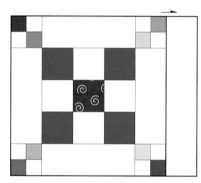

Make 11.

2. Sew 2" blue sashing squares to one end of six 2" x 10½" white sashing strips. Press toward the sashing strips.

Make 6.

3. Pin and sew the sashing strips with squares to the bottoms of six blocks with side sashing. Press.

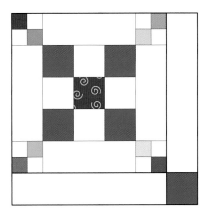

Make 6.

4. Arrange the block units as shown. Sew into horizontal rows and join the rows.

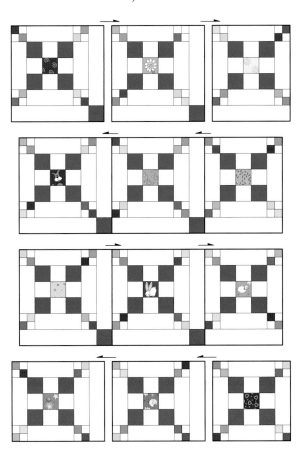

5. Referring to "Straight-Cut Borders" on page 17, measure, trim, and sew the 1½" white inner-border strips first to the top and bottom edges of the quilt top and then to the side edges. Repeat for the 3" blue outer-border strips.

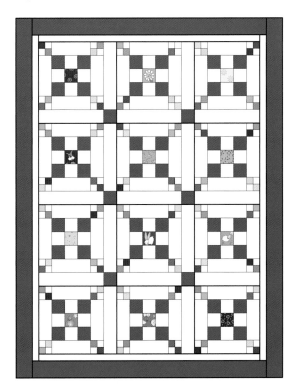

6. Assemble the quilt sandwich as indicated in "Quiltmaking Basics" (page 18). Quilt as desired. Bind the edges using the white strips; add a label.

Snowball

42" x 54"

The flexibility of the Snowball block makes it fun to work with. It makes a wonderful scrap quilt, but it is also beautiful made with fabrics from a single color family, as in "Block in a Box" (page 29) or made with fewer fabrics such as in "Simple Nine Patch" (page 67).

- **Skill level:** beginner ●
● 48 blocks, 6" finished size ●
● 24 A blocks ●
● 24 B blocks ●
● 1" inner border ●
● 2" outer border ●

Materials

Yardages are based on 42"-wide fabric.

1⅝ yards *total* of assorted bright fabrics for blocks

1⅛ yards of white fabric for blocks and inner border

½ yard of blue fabric for outer border

½ yard of red fabric for binding

2⅞ yards of fabric for backing

46" x 58" piece of batting

Single Block A Requirements

9 bright squares, 2½" x 2½"

Single Block B Requirements

4 bright squares, 2½" x 2½"
1 white square, 6½" x 6½"

Cutting

All measurements include ¼"-wide seam allowances.

From the assorted bright fabrics, cut:

- 312 squares, 2½" x 2½"

From the white fabric, cut:

- 24 squares, 6½" x 6½"
- 5 strips, 1½" x 42"

From the blue fabric, cut:

- 5 strips, 2½" x 42"

From the red fabric, cut:

- 6 strips, 2½" x 42"

Assembling the Blocks

1. Sew 2½" bright squares into 72 pairs. Press to the left side. Sew another 2½" bright square to the end of each pair of bright squares. Press to the left.

Make 72.

2. Divide the pieced strips into groups of three. Rotate the center strips so that the seam allowances are pointing to the right, rather than the left. This will make it easier to match seams when pinning. Pin and sew the top and center strips together, being careful to match seams. Press toward the center strip. Pin and sew the remaining strip to the bottom of the pieced unit, matching seams. Press toward the center strip.

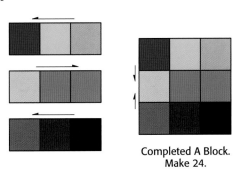

Completed A Block.
Make 24.

3. For the B blocks, draw a diagonal line from corner to corner on the wrong side of each of the 96 remaining 2½" assorted squares. Align a 2½" bright square with the upper-right corner of each 6½" white square, right sides together, as shown. Sew on the diagonal line. Trim the excess fabric ¼" from the stitching line. Press toward the bright corner.

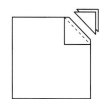

4. In the same manner, stitch a 2½" bright square to each of the remaining corners to complete the B blocks.

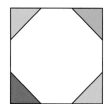

Completed B Block.
Make 24.

Assembling and Finishing the Quilt Top

1. Pin and sew the A and B blocks into pairs. Press toward the A blocks.

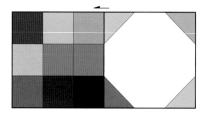

Make 24.

2. Divide the block pairs into two groups. Arrange them so that in one group block A is on the left, and in the other group block A is on the right.

Pin pairs together, matching seams, and sew. Press.

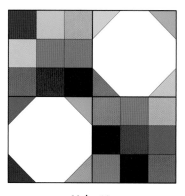

Make 12.

3. Arrange the 12 large blocks as shown. Sew into horizontal rows and join the rows together.

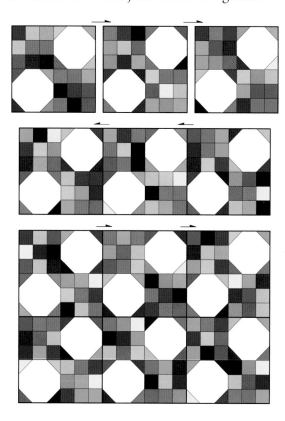

4. Referring to "Straight-Cut Borders" on page 17, measure, trim, and sew the 1½" white inner-border strips first to the top and bottom edges of the quilt top and then to the side edges. Repeat with the 3" blue outer-border strips.

5. Assemble the quilt sandwich as indicated in "Quiltmaking Basics" (page 18). Quilt as desired. Bind the edges using the red strips; add a label.

Summer Winds

46" x 59½"

Bright triangles provide a great deal of movement in the finished quilt. While large-scale novelty fabrics don't work well for this quilt, it provides an excellent opportunity for using the leftover scraps from fussy cutting.

- ● **Skill level:** intermediate ●
- ● 12 blocks, 12" finished size ●
- ● 1½" sashing ●
- ● 1" inner border ●
- ● 2½" outer border ●

Materials

Yardages are based on 42"-wide fabric.

2⅝ yards of white fabric for blocks and sashing

1¾ yards *total* of assorted bright fabrics for blocks

⅝ yard of blue fabric for sashing squares and outer border

¼ yard of purple fabric for inner border

½ yard of pink fabric for binding

3⅛ yards of fabric for backing

50" x 64" piece of batting

Single Block Requirements

6 white squares, 3½" x 3½"

6 bright squares, 3½" x 3½"

8 white squares, 2½" x 2½"

4 bright rectangles, 2½" x 4½"

4 white rectangles, 2½" x 4½"

4 bright squares, 2½" x 2½"

1 white square, 4½" x 4½"

Cutting

All measurements include ¼"-wide seam allowances.

From the white fabric, cut:

- ● 72 squares, 3½" x 3½"
- ● 96 squares, 2½" x 2½"
- ● 48 rectangles, 2½" x 4½"
- ● 12 squares, 4½" x 4½"
- ● 17 rectangles, 2" x 12½"

From the assorted bright fabrics, cut:

- ● 72 squares, 3½" x 3½"
- ● 48 rectangles, 2½" x 4½"
- ● 48 squares, 2½" x 2½"

From the blue fabric, cut:

- ● 6 squares, 2" x 2"
- ● 5 strips, 3" x 42"

From the purple fabric, cut:

- ● 5 strips, 1½" x 42"

From the pink fabric, cut:

- ● 6 strips, 2½" x 42"

Assembling the Blocks

1. Sew the 3½" white squares and bright squares together to make 144 half-square-triangle units (see "Half-Square-Triangle Units," page 14). Trim to 2½".

Make 144.

2. Draw a diagonal line on the wrong side of the 2½" white squares. Referring to the illustration, position a white square over one corner

of 48 bright 2½" x 4½" rectangles, right sides together. Sew on the drawn line. Trim ¼" from the sewn line. Press toward the corner.

3. Align another 2½" white square with the other side of each rectangle, as shown. Sew on the drawn line and trim ¼" from the stitching. Press toward the corner to make 48 flying-geese units.

Flying-geese unit.
Make 48.

4. Pin and sew a 2½" x 4½" white rectangle to each of the flying-geese units as shown. Press toward the white rectangle.

Make 48.

5. Sew a 2½" half-square-triangle unit to each of the 48 bright 2½" squares as shown. Press toward the bright squares.

Make 48.

6. Sew the remaining 96 half-square-triangle units into pairs and press as shown.

Make 48.

7. Pin and sew the units from step 6 to the tops of the units from step 5, matching seams, to make 48 corner units. Press as shown. Set aside.

Corner unit.
Make 48.

8. Pin and sew 24 units from step 4 to opposite sides of the 4½" white squares, as shown, to make center units. Press toward the center squares.

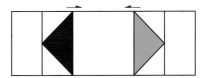

Center unit.
Make 12.

9. Pin and sew the corner units to opposite sides of the 24 remaining flying-geese squares from step 4, as shown, to make top and bottom units. Press toward the corner units.

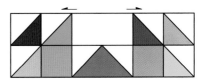

Top/bottom unit.
Make 24.

10. Pin and sew the top and bottom units to opposite sides of the center units, matching seams. Press.

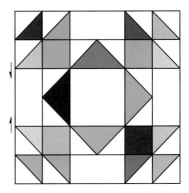

Completed block.
Make 12.

Assembling and Finishing the Quilt Top

1. Pin and sew 2" x 12½" white sashing strips to the right sides of all but one of the completed blocks. Press toward the sashing strips.

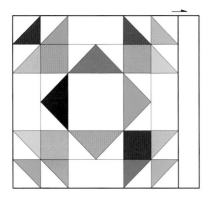

Make 11.

2. Sew 2" blue sashing squares to one end of six of the 2" x 12½" white sashing strips. Press toward the sashing strips.

Make 6.

3. Pin and sew the sashing strips with squares to the bottoms of six of the blocks with side sashing. Press.

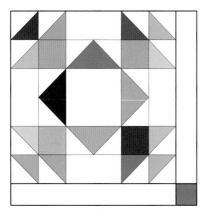

Make 6.

4. Arrange the block units as shown. Sew into horizontal rows and join the rows.

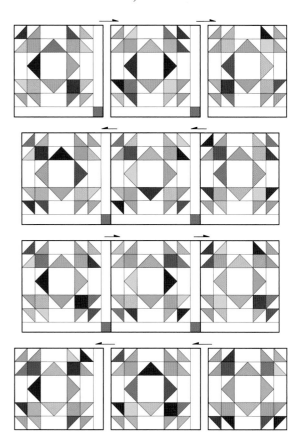

5. Referring to "Straight-Cut Borders" on page 17, measure, trim, and sew the 1½" purple inner-border strips first to the top and bottom edges of the quilt top and then to the side edges. Repeat with the 3" blue outer-border strips.

6. Assemble the quilt sandwich as indicated in "Quiltmaking Basics" (page 18). Quilt as desired. Bind the edges using the pink strips; add a label.

Swirling Stars

45" x 57"

The background fabric that you select will play a large role in the mood of the finished quilt. Changing the white background shown here to dark blue or black would provide a nighttime-sky setting for the stars and bring an added intensity to the colors.

Materials

Yardages are based on 42"-wide fabric.

2⅛ yards of white fabric for blocks

1½ yards *total* of assorted bright fabrics for blocks

⅝ yard of blue fabric for outer border

½ yard of purple fabric for sashing and inner border

½ yard of multicolored fabric for binding

3 yards of fabric for backing

49" x 61" piece of batting

Single Block Requirements

2 bright squares, 3½" x 3½"

2 white squares, 3½" x 3½"

1 bright square, 2½" x 2½"

4 white squares, 2½" x 2½"

Cutting

All measurements include ¼"-wide seam allowances.

From the white fabric, cut:

- 96 squares, 3½" x 3½"
- 192 squares, 2½" x 2½"

From the assorted bright fabrics, cut:

- 96 squares, 3½" x 3½"
- 48 squares, 2½" x 2½"

From the purple fabric, cut:

- 10 strips, 1½" x 42"

From the blue fabric, cut:

- 5 strips, 3" x 42"

From the multicolored fabric, cut:

- 6 strips, 2½" x 42"*

*If the fabric is wide enough after prewashing, you made need only 5 strips of fabric.

Assembling the Blocks

1. Using the 3½" white squares and bright squares, assemble 192 half-square-triangle units (see "Half-Square-Triangle Units," page 14). Trim to 2½".

Make 192.

2. Sew half-square-triangle units to opposite sides of 48 bright 2½" squares as shown. Press toward the bright squares.

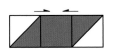

Center unit.
Make 48.

3. Sew 2½" white squares to opposite sides of the half-square-triangle units to make 96 top and bottom units. Press toward the white squares.

Top/bottom unit.
Make 96.

4. Pin the top and bottom units to the center units as shown, matching seams, and sew. Press seam allowances toward the bottom of each unit.

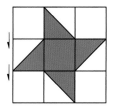

Completed star block.
Make 48.

Assembling and Finishing the Quilt Top

1. Set aside four completed Star blocks. Divide the remaining blocks into two groups. Rotate one group 180° so that the seam allowances are pointing upward. The other group should have the seam allowances pointing downward. Pin and sew the blocks into 22 pairs. Press.

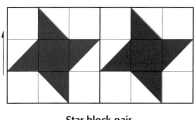

Star block pair.
Make 22.

2. Pin and sew 12 units from step 1 into pairs, matching seams, to make a four-block units as shown. Press.

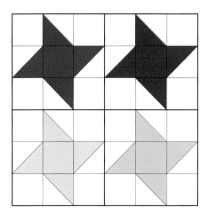

Make 6.

3. Pin and sew the four-block units into pairs to make horizontal sections. Join the sections to make the center Star block panel.

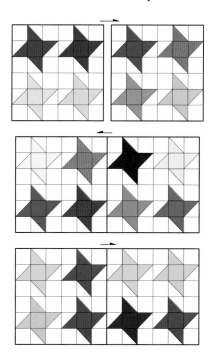

4. Pin and sew the remaining Star block pairs into two strips of four stars and two strips of six stars.

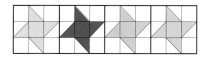

Four-star strip.
Make 2.

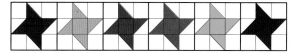

Six-star strip.
Make 2.

5. Pin and sew a 1½" purple sashing strip to the bottom edge of each of the six-star strips. Press toward the sashing. Trim the sashing strips so that they are even with the left and right edges of the block strips.

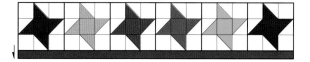

6. Pin and sew the long star strips to opposite sides of the large center star panel as shown. Press toward the sashing strips.

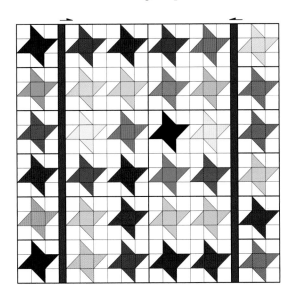

7. Cut one of the remaining 1½" purple strips into 4 pieces, 6½" long. Pin and sew a 1½" x 6½" purple sashing strip to one side of each of the four remaining individual blocks. Press toward the sashing strips.

Make 4.

8. Pin and sew the stars with sashing to opposite ends of the four-star strips as shown. Press toward the sashing strips.

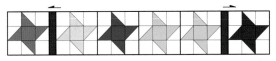

Make 2.

9. Sew a 1½" purple sashing strip to the bottom edge of each strip unit from step 8. Press toward the sashing just added. Trim the sashing strips

so that they are even with the left and right edges of the strip units.

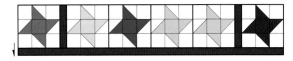

Make 2.

10. Pin and sew the units from step 9 to the top and bottom edges of the center star panel. When pinning, make sure to align the vertical sashing strips on the center section with the vertical sashing strips on the top and bottom units as shown. Press toward the sashing strips.

11. Referring to "Straight-Cut Borders" on page 17, measure, trim, and sew the 1½" purple inner-border strips first to the top and bottom edges of the quilt top and then to the side edges. Repeat with the 3" blue outer-border strips.

12. Assemble the quilt sandwich as indicated in "Quiltmaking Basics" (page 18). Quilt as desired. Bind the edges using the multicolored strips; add a label.

Unequal Double Irish Chain

41" x 53"

The 3" fussy-cut squares that form the center chain provide a focus for this quilt. All the fussy-cut squares were taken from a single fabric, but the same effect could be maintained with a wide variety of fussy-cut fabrics, as long as you unified them by using a single fabric for the second chain.

Skill level: beginner
- 48 blocks, 6" finished size
- 24 A blocks
- 24 B blocks
- 2½" border

Materials

Yardages are based on 42"-wide fabric.

1½ yards of dark purple fabric for blocks and border

1⅜ yards of light purple fabric for blocks and binding

¾ yard of blue fabric for blocks*

2¾ yards of fabric for backing

45" x 57" piece of batting

The fabric requirement listed here is for straight-cut fabric. If you want to fussy cut your quilt, see "Fussy Cutting" on page 12. You may need to purchase double this amount of fabric or more.

Single Block A Requirements

1 blue square, 3½" x 3½"

4 blue squares, 2" x 2"

4 dark purple rectangles, 2" x 3½"

Single Block B Requirements

4 dark purple squares, 2" x 2"

2 light purple rectangles, 2" x 3½"

1 light purple rectangle, 3½" x 6½"

Cutting

All measurements include ¼"-wide seam allowances.

From the dark purple fabric, cut:
- 96 rectangles, 2" x 3½"
- 96 squares, 2" x 2"
- 5 strips, 3" x 42"

From the blue fabric, cut:
- 24 squares, 3½" x 3½"
- 96 squares, 2" x 2"

From the light purple fabric, cut:
- 48 rectangles, 2" x 3½"
- 24 rectangles, 3½" x 6½"
- 5 strips, 2½" x 42"

Assembling the Blocks

1. To assemble block A, sew 2" x 3½" dark purple rectangles to opposite sides of the 24 blue 3½" squares. Press toward the dark purple fabric.

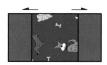

Center unit.
Make 24.

2. In the same manner, sew 2" blue squares to opposite ends of the 48 remaining 2" x 3½" dark purple rectangles. Press toward the dark purple rectangles.

Top/bottom unit.
Make 48.

3. Pin and sew the top and bottom units to the center units, matching seams as shown. Press toward the center.

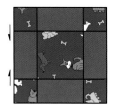

Completed A block.
Make 24.

4. To assemble block B, sew a 2" dark purple square to one end of each 2" x 3½" light purple rectangle. Press toward the dark purple squares. Repeat on the opposite end of the light purple rectangles.

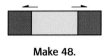

Make 48.

5. Pin and sew the strips from step 5 to opposite sides of the 3½" x 6½" light purple rectangles as shown to complete block B. Press toward the pieced strips.

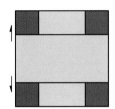

Completed B block.
Make 24.

Tip

If you fussy cut your fabric, you'll need to make sure that your blocks are all oriented in the correct direction before you begin to sew the A and B blocks together.

Assembling and Finishing the Quilt Top

1. Pin and sew the A and B blocks into 24 pairs. Press toward the A blocks.

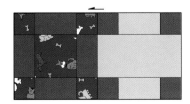

Make 24.

2. Divide the block pairs into two groups and arrange them so that in one group block A is on the left, and in the other group block A is on the right. Pin and sew into four-block units, matching seams. Press.

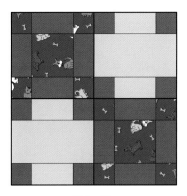

Make 12.

3. Arrange the four-block units into horizontal rows. Join the rows.

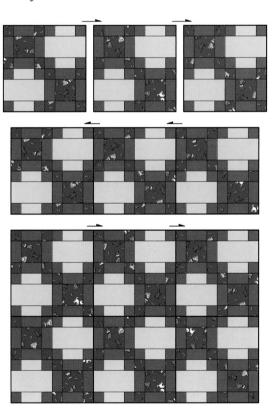

4. Referring to "Straight-Cut Borders" on page 17, measure, trim, and sew the 3" dark purple border strips first to the top and bottom edges of the quilt top and then to the side edges.

5. Assemble the quilt sandwich as indicated in "Quiltmaking Basics" (page 18). Quilt as desired. Bind the edges using the light purple strips; add a label.

Unequal Irish Chain

48" x 60"

The bright colors and large areas of cream give this quilt a light and airy quality.
A smaller version of this quilt, five blocks by five blocks, makes a wonderful baby quilt.

Materials

Yardages are based on 42"-wide fabric.

2¼ yards of cream fabric for blocks

⅞ yard *total* of assorted bright fabrics for blocks

¾ yard of blue fabric for border

½ yard of green fabric for binding

3¼ yards of backing fabric

52" x 64" piece of batting

Single Block A Requirements

4 cream rectangles, 2" x 3½"

1 bright square, 3½" x 3½"

4 bright squares, 2" x 2"

Single Block B Requirements

1 cream square, 6½" x 6½"

Cutting

All measurements include ¼"-wide seam allowances.

From the cream fabric, cut:

- 128 rectangles, 2" x 3½"
- 31 squares, 6½" x 6½"

From the assorted bright fabrics, cut:

- 32 squares, 3½" x 3½"
- 128 squares, 2" x 2"

From the blue fabric, cut:

- 6 strips, 3½" x 42"

From the green fabric, cut:

- 6 strips, 2½" x 42"

● ● ● ● ● ● ● ● Tip ● ● ● ● ● ● ● ●

This quilt is beautiful when made with fussy-cut novelty fabrics. Consider gathering your favorite novelties for this one.

Assembling the Blocks

1. To assemble block A, sew 2" x 3½" cream rectangles to opposite sides of the 3½" bright squares. Press toward the bright squares.

Center unit.
Make 32.

2. In the same manner, sew the 2" bright squares to opposite ends of the remaining 2" x 3½" cream rectangles to make 64 top and bottom units. Press toward the bright squares.

Top/bottom unit.
Make 64.

3. Pin and sew the top and bottom units to the center units, matching seams, as shown. Press.

Completed A block.
Make 32.

Tip

If you fussy cut your fabric, some motifs may be directional. Before you begin to sew the A and B blocks together, you'll need to make sure that your fabrics are all oriented in the correct direction.

Assembling and Finishing the Quilt Top

1. Set aside five A blocks and four 6½" cream B blocks. Pin and sew the remaining blocks into pairs as shown, paying attention to directional fabric. Make 15 A-B pairs and 12 B-A pairs. Press toward the B blocks.

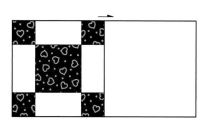

A-B pair.
Make 15.

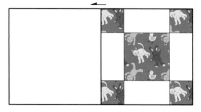

B-A pair.
Make 12.

2. Pin and sew the five remaining A blocks to five of the A-B pairs, creating A-B-A units. Press toward the B blocks.

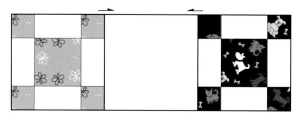

Make 5.

3. Pin and sew the remaining B blocks to four of the B-A pairs, creating B-A-B units. Press toward the B blocks.

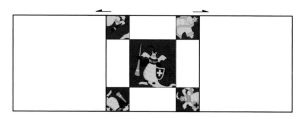

Make 4.

4. Pin and sew the A-B-A and B-A-B units into pairs as shown. There will be one extra A-B-A unit. Press.

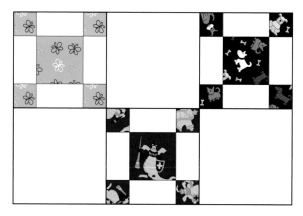

Make 4.

5. Pin and sew A-B and B-A pairs into large blocks as shown. There will be two extra A-B pairs. Press.

Make 8.

6. Arrange the block units as shown. Sew the units into horizontal rows. Join the rows.

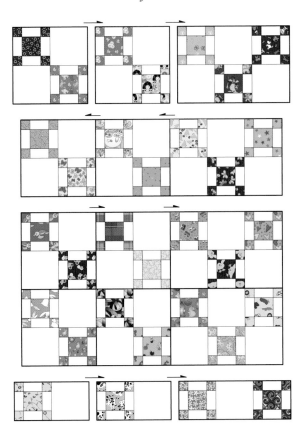

7. Referring to "Straight-Cut Borders" on page 17, measure, trim, and sew the 3½" blue inner-border strips first to the top and bottom edges of the quilt top and then to the side edges.

8. Assemble the quilt sandwich as indicated in "Quiltmaking Basics" (page 18). Quilt as desired. Bind the edges using the green strips; add a label.

X's and O's

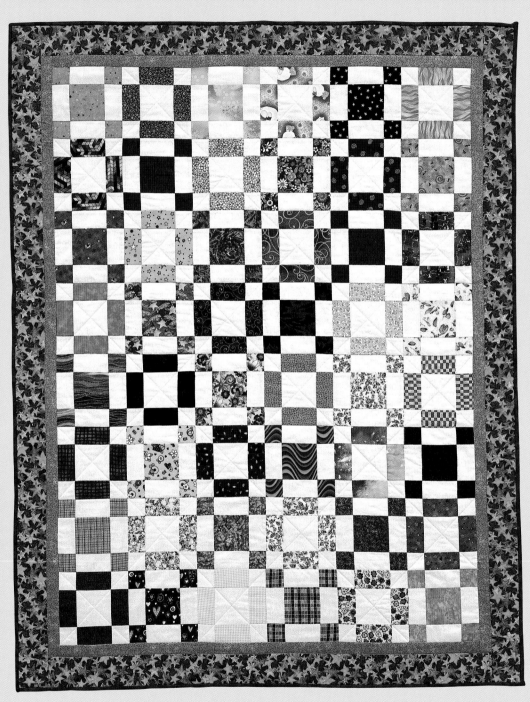

41" x 55"

The X's and O's in this quilt are made by reversing the bright fabrics and background fabrics. If you have a limited number of fabrics available, try making one X block and one O block from each fabric and place the blocks randomly in the quilt design. Some lucky child will have fun trying to match up the different block pairs.

- **Skill level:** beginner ●
- 48 blocks, 6" finished size ●
- 24 of block X ●
- 24 of block O ●
- 1" inner border ●
- 2½" outer border ●

Materials

Yardages are based on 42"-wide fabric.

1⅜ yards *total* of assorted bright fabrics for blocks

1⅜ yards of cream fabric for blocks

½ yard of blue star fabric for outer border

¼ yard of purple fabric for inner border

½ yard of dark blue fabric for binding

2¾ yards of fabric for backing

45" x 59" piece of batting

Single Block X Requirements

1 bright square, 3½" x 3½"

4 cream rectangles, 2" x 3½"

4 bright squares, 2" x 2"

Single Block O Requirements

1 cream square, 3½" x 3½"

4 bright rectangles, 2" x 3½"

4 cream squares, 2" x 2"

Cutting

All measurements include ¼"-wide seam allowances.

From the cream fabric, cut:

- 96 rectangles, 2" x 3½"
- 24 squares, 3½" x 3½"
- 96 squares, 2" x 2"

From the assorted bright fabrics, cut:

- 24 squares, 3½" x 3½"
- 96 squares, 2" x 2"
- 96 rectangles, 2" x 3½"

From the purple fabric, cut:

- 5 strips, 1½" x 42"

From the blue star fabric, cut:

- 5 strips, 3" x 42"

From the dark blue fabric, cut:

- 6 strips, 2½" x 42"

Assembling the Blocks

1. To assemble block X, sew a 2" x 3½" cream rectangle to the 3½" bright squares as shown. Press toward the bright squares. Make 24.

Make 24.

2. Sew a 2" x 3½" cream rectangle to each unit from step 1, as shown, to make center units. Press toward the bright squares.

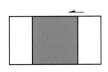

Center unit.
Make 24.

3. In the same manner, sew 2" bright squares to opposite ends of the remaining 2" x 3½" cream rectangles. Press toward the bright squares.

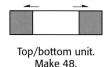

Top/bottom unit.
Make 48.

4. Pin and sew the top and bottom units to the center units, matching seams. Press toward the center units.

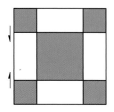

Completed X block.
Make 24.

5. To assemble block O, repeat steps 1–4, replacing cream fabric with bright, and bright fabric with cream. In step 4, press toward the top and bottom units.

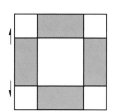

Completed O block.
Make 24.

Assembling and Finishing the Quilt Top

1. Pin and sew blocks X and O into 24 pairs. Press toward the X blocks.

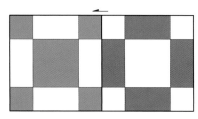

Make 24.

2. Divide the 24 block pairs into two groups and align so that in one pile block X is on the left, and in the other pile block X is on the right.

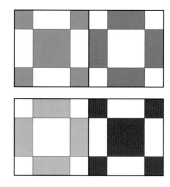

3. Pin and sew the block pairs into 12 four-block units. Press.

4. Arrange the four-block units as shown. Sew into horizontal rows and join the rows.

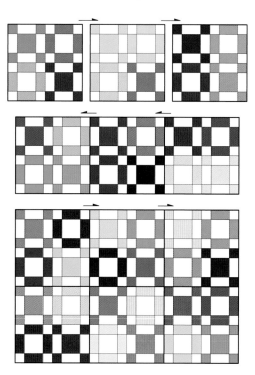

5. Referring to "Straight-Cut Borders" on page 17, measure, trim, and sew the 1½" purple inner-border strips first to the top and bottom edges of the quilt top and then to the side edges. Repeat with the 3" outer-border strips.

6. Assemble the quilt sandwich as indicated in "Quiltmaking Basics" (page 18). Quilt as desired. Bind the edges of the quilt using the dark blue strips; add a label.

Charitable Organizations

ABC Quilts
569 First NH Turnpike #3
Northwood, NH 03261
1-800-536-5694
info@abcquilts.org
www.abcquilts.org
This organization provides hand-made quilts to children who are HIV-positive or affected by drugs or alcohol.

Binky Patrol Inc.
PO Box 1468
Laguna Beach, CA 92652-1468
(949) 916-5926
binky@binkypatrol.org
www.binkypatrol.org
This national organization distributes blankets to children and teens in need. Local chapter information is available on their Web site.

Catholic Community Services
100 23rd Ave. S.
Seattle, WA 98144-2302
(206) 328-5696
info@ccsww.org
www.ccsww.org
This is the Catholic Community Services (CCS) information for western Washington. CCS offices around the country can be located on the internet or by contacting your local diocese. CCS provides a variety of services for people and families in need.

Project Linus
PO Box 5621
Bloomington, IL 61702-5621
(309) 664-7814
information@projectlinus.org
www.projectlinus.org
A list of local chapters can be found on the national organization's Web page or by contacting them directly.

Quilt for a Cause
Jeannie Beahan
5083 N. Pinnacle Cove Dr.
Tucson, AZ 85749
(520) 529-5723
jeabea@msn.com
www.quiltforacause.org
This organization accepts quilts for a live and silent auction to raise money to help fight breast and gynecological cancer.

Quilts 4 Cancer
PO Box 4702
Pahrump, NV 89041
(775) 751-5356
barb@quilts4cancer.com
www.quilts4cancer.com
In conjunction with Candlelighters Childhood Cancer Foundation, this organization provides quilts for children with cancer.

Quilts from the Heart
9231 Baring Way
Everett, WA 98208-2442
qfth@quiltsfromtheheart.org
www.quiltsfromtheheart.org
This group makes and donates quilts to small organizations serving "at risk" children, teens, and adults in western Washington State. Its membership has grown to more than 100 since its founding in 1993. In that time, over 2,400 quilts have been donated to more than 20 recipient organizations.

Wrap Them in Love
2522-A Old Hwy 99S
Mt. Vernon, WA 98273
admin@wraptheminlove.org
www.wraptheminlove.org
This organization donates quilts to children living in orphanages around the world.

YWCA
1015 18th St. NW, Ste. 1100
Washington, DC 20036
(202) 467-0801
info@ywca.org
www.ywca.org
Local chapters support various projects such as transitional housing and shelters for the homeless and victims of domestic violence.

Karin Renaud was born and raised in western Washington. She studied speech language pathology at Washington State University, earning an MA in 1986. Karin married her husband, Matt, in 1990, and has been quilting for nearly as long as she's been married. While visiting her husband's family in 1990, Karin learned to quilt from a family friend, Kelly Kampmann, who donated her time, talent, patience, and even her fabric. When Karin received her first quilting supplies as a Christmas gift from her mother-in-law, Margaret Renaud, she was hooked. She has been making quilts for charity for almost as long as she's been quilting; since 2001 she has made and donated more than 30 quilts to Project Linus.

Karin and her husband live in Enumclaw, Washington, with their children, Luke and Kaitlyn, and two springer spaniels, Beau and Amy. In addition to quilting, Karin enjoys reading, walking, and watching baseball, especially the Seattle Mariners.

Acknowledgments

I would like to thank several people who have been instrumental in getting this book completed. Kaitlyn Renaud, Diane and Cory Olson, and Brit Nelson were all willing pattern testers and proof-readers. Your insights were extremely helpful.

My Sirius 4-H quilters: Emily Foley, Willow Foley, Chris Sechrist, Gabby Sechrist, and Lauren Sechrist—all of whom helped me clarify things for myself as I explained things to them.

Linda Johnson, author of *Pink Lemonade and Other Delights,* and Mary Stanton, owner of The Calico Cat and Bernina Too! for their encouragement and support.

Lynn Mazer, coordinator of the South Puget Sound chapter of Project Linus, and Carol Babbitt, president of Project Linus, for their assistance as well as for all the work they do for children.

Kristin Lipke-Eberly and Lynn Larrigan, two women who have always encouraged me to attempt anything, and cheered me on as I did it.

The wonderful staff at Martingale for the assistance and expertise that made this book a reality.

Thank you to my kids, Luke and Kaitlyn, for putting up with my absorption in this project, including my quilting on the dining-room table before breakfast.

And most of all to my husband, Matt, for endlessly listening to my ideas, looking at my quilts, helping out in dozens of ways, and above all for never complaining about how much I spent on fabric!